THE INVISIBILITY CURE

HOW TO STAND OUT, GET NOTICED AND GET WHAT YOU WANT AT WORK

CHRISSY SCIVICQUE

CCS VENTURES, LLC (WWW.EATYOURCAREER.COM)

For you ... yes YOU
This book is dedicated to you, dear reader. May you always be seen,
heard, and valued. You deserve it.

CONTENTS

THE INVISIBLE INTERN

Many years ago, when I was working as an intern during my sophomore year of college, I had my first memorable experience with feeling invisible at work.

As a business student at Sonoma State University in California, I had landed a gig with one of the largest and most prestigious wine distributors in the region. My job was to perform statistical analysis on the seasonality of sales. Don't worry; it sounds fancier than it really was.

I was hired in mid-September, right at the very beginning of the school year. This was my first "real" job in the professional world and, as the sole intern, I immediately struggled to interact with my colleagues. In meetings and around the office, they mostly ignored me. I was afraid to ask questions because, whenever I did, they spoke down to me and did little to hide their annoyance. Eventually, I decided my best course of action was to keep my head down and cause as little disruption as possible.

Still, I reliably showed up three days a week for the entire first semester of school. I figured out the work I needed to accomplish because no one else seemed to know. I told myself I was doing a good job, even though I had received no direct feedback. I desperately wanted to list this job on my incredibly sparse resume, so I bit the bullet and figured this was all totally normal.

Then one day in mid-December, while sitting in my corner cubicle, silently working away, I overhead a conversation.

My co-workers were talking about the company holiday party. They were discussing the venue and who they were bringing. And suddenly I realized: The party was happening *that night*.

I hadn't been invited.

Not a single person had thought to tell me about the party. Later, my boss confirmed that it wasn't intentional or malicious. It truly was an oversight. I had simply been forgotten. For some reason, that hurt even more than if it had been a deliberate slight.

I packed up my things and went home early that day so I could cry to my roommates about my horrible treatment.

Naturally, no one at the office even noticed I had left.

While my situation might have been a little more blatant than most, the feeling of being "invisible" is painfully common in the workplace. It can manifest in a number of ways. For example:

- Your work goes unacknowledged and unappreciated.

- Your opinions and ideas are never sought by others.
- When you express your opinions or ideas (unsolicited), others don't listen.
- You aren't included in projects where your expertise would clearly be useful.
- You are continuously overlooked when it comes to recognition, rewards, and advancement opportunities—despite being deserving.

When you're experiencing these things, it's easy to see yourself as the victim. But that attitude does little to help. Instead, you have to be willing to look at your part.

In my situation, I was young and inexperienced. To be fair, the company I was working for had no idea how to support an intern, and the people there were too busy to care much about me. But I had allowed fear and discomfort to force me into the shadows. *I had turned myself invisible.* I could hardly blame my co-workers for the missing party invitation when I had literally been hiding in my little workspace for months, avoiding interaction as much as possible.

Most people can relate to my feelings of fear and discomfort, but the hiding that happens is usually more figurative. I've found that even the most experienced professionals struggle to put themselves "out there." They fail to speak up as often as they'd like. They don't self-promote the way they know they should. They rarely branch out to build new strategic relationships with colleagues.

These things all contribute to that feeling of invisibility. After all, in a busy workplace, it's easy to get lost in the crowd. **Just keeping your head down and doing your job isn't enough to get noticed.** You have to be willing to face the fear and discomfort that comes with stepping out of the shadows and shining a spotlight on yourself.

But you also have to do it in the right way.

After the holiday party fiasco, I vowed to never be invisible at work again. In the years immediately following, I found myself pulled to the other end of the spectrum. In trying to make myself visible, I came off as loud, bossy, overly opinionated, arrogant, and at times, aggressive. I refused to stay quiet, even when that would have been the appropriate behavior. I told myself it was better to occasionally be seen in a bad light than to not be seen at all; a bad reputation is better than none.

That rationale was, of course, utter nonsense. My behavior ultimately backfired, making me *hyper*visible—an equally dangerous condition. Soon, I found myself perpetually under a microscope, unable to do anything right. Everything I did or said was misunderstood. My boss watched me like a hawk, ready to pounce on any wrong move. Around the watercooler, I just knew people were whispering, *"Can you believe what she did now?"*

This was yet another form of invisibility; I still wasn't being seen for who or what I *really* was. I was getting attention all right, but the wrong kind. I had put myself in a box through my own misguided actions, and I had no idea how to break free.

Being hypervisible may look different from being invisible, but the underlying feelings are the same: isolation, inferiority, injustice. Likewise, the career consequences are just as grave. Again, it's easy to point the finger at others, but we must look at our own part if we wish to improve the situation. Much of the time, visibility problems are the result of individual behavior, which is good news because it means each individual has the power to change their experience. In an organization where *every* person has a genuine and equal opportunity to succeed, your actions (for better or worse) dictate your level of visibility or lack thereof.

I'll pause here quickly to acknowledge that, at times, there may indeed be other contributing factors at play. Institutional racism, sexism, and other discriminatory practices unfairly marginalize certain groups of people. Making a person feel hypervisible or invisible, whether consciously or subconsciously, is certainly a common intimidation tactic. In such cases, gaining visibility may require a change of environment.

Research shows that women tend to struggle more than their male counterparts when it comes to gaining visibility. I believe this is largely due to the preconceived notions some of us women were raised with—that we should only speak when spoken to, that it's not polite to talk about ourselves, that we should be agreeable and compliant. The skills we have to leverage to truly distinguish ourselves in the workplace often feel in direct violation of these unspoken rules.

We'll address many things throughout this book, including smashing some of those old ways of thinking. Whether you're a man or a woman, if you're reading this book, it's probably safe to assume that you have some beliefs that aren't serving you. It's time to examine what those are and get rid of anything that's holding you back.

Thankfully, with the help of experience and several influential mentors, I was able to find my footing in the professional world before too much damage had been done. I figured out who I was and who I wanted to be. I discovered the power of perceptions and how I could influence them ... in ways that helped me or ways that harmed me.

With practice, I learned how to be a vocal advocate for myself without appearing self-righteous. I learned how to confidently express alternative points of view without alienating others. I learned when to shut up and when to speak up; when to stand up and when to back down.

Once I had mastered these skills, I finally felt seen—*in the right way and for the right reasons.* My work was respected and rewarded. When I spoke, people listened. I felt like a valuable member of the team, rather than some sidelined player.

The curse of invisibility had lifted.

These days, as a career coach and corporate trainer, I often share my experiences with my clients. I find that most professionals can relate in one way or another. Striking the right balance in the workplace, embodying both confidence and humility, *simultaneously*, is tough. It's easy to fall too far to one side or the other and become too big or too small.

Just like Goldilocks, we're all looking for that "just right" amount and kind of visibility.

I've come a long way from the days of being the Invisible Intern. Over the years, I've come to understand that genuine visibility is like a lot of things in the professional world—it's a privilege, not a right. It's not automatically granted simply by virtue of showing up. You have to earn it. Those who expect something for nothing in the workplace are doomed to be disappointed.

These days, I run my own coaching and training business, and I specialize in working with people who feel marginalized in the corporate world. Many (though certainly not all) of my clients are women, and I tend to work with lots of folks in administrative roles—assistants and other support staff. As both a woman and a former admin, I can deeply appreciate the challenges these clients face.

However, no matter who I'm working with or in what capacity, I always emphasize the fact that I'm not perfect. I've made mistakes in my career and I've learned to overcome them. I do this work because I know what it's like to feel invisible, and I also know it doesn't have to be a permanent condition.

This book's goal is to eradicate the disease of invisibility once and for all—to provide a cure that will forever change the way you present yourself in the workplace and, thus, the way others see you and treat you. It's no exaggeration to say that this cure has the power to completely change your experience at work.

However, the cure is not as simple as taking a pill. It is a multistep protocol that requires your full participation. I'm providing the instructions, but you have to follow them as prescribed.

In Chapter 2, you'll learn the essential ingredients that, when mixed together, create the magic elixir. In Chapter 3, you'll discover the hidden mental barriers you must overcome to ensure the potion works.

The rest of the book will teach you specific strategies to set yourself up for success. These are the tactical tools you need to eliminate the pain of invisibility once and for all, and immunize yourself for the future.

Throughout these pages, I share a variety of stories to help illustrate the concepts I present. Many of these are my own personal experiences, though some come from my coaching and training clients. At least one comes from a participant in my monthly Q&A session. For any story that is not mine, I have changed the name of the individual to protect his or her privacy.

~

Note: You can sign up to get notified about my upcoming FREE monthly Q&A sessions and training webinars by visiting EatYourCareer.com/signup

~

AT TIMES, you may find my recommendations too delicate. At others, you may feel I'm too brash. But I stand behind everything in this book. I have personally employed these strategies with great success as have *hundreds* of my coaching and training clients.

Finally, I want to be clear: While I use the somewhat silly analogy of a magic elixir that will cure your visibility concerns in the workplace, there is nothing mystical about my methods. Everything you learn here can and should be applied in the real world.

Even if I had a magic wand that could give you exactly what you want without doing the hard work required, I wouldn't use it. I believe the effort you are willing to put in dictates your results. It also makes the entire process much more satisfying. If it were too easy, it wouldn't be special. That's why this book is necessary.

Many people won't do the work required to achieve the results. Don't be one of them. Just knowing the prescription doesn't make you well. If you're able to rise to the challenge and follow my course of treatment, you will stand out, get noticed, and get what you want at work. That is my promise to you.

2

THE FUNDAMENTALS OF VISIBILITY

Being "visible" at work is about more than simply being seen and heard. It's about standing out in a positive and memorable way. Today's workplace is competitive, crowded, and fast-moving. People who blend in are easily overlooked and quickly forgotten. To make a name for yourself, you have to be willing to do things that others *aren't* doing—whether that's because they're afraid, or complacent, or because they just don't know any better.

Being truly visible in this way is a requirement for achieving your career goals, whatever they may be. Invisible people don't get the choice assignments. They don't earn raises or promotions.

Visibility also provides a measure of security. When times are tight and tough decisions have to be made, invisible people are the easiest to let go. Their absence causes practically no disruption. Few people care or even notice.

Those who are most visible are, in fact, somewhat protected

in difficult times. Their absence would almost certainly cause a disruption. People would notice! People would care! The decision to remove a highly visible individual is not made lightly and, quite often, deliberate steps are taken specifically to avoid it.

If circumstances are such that it can't be avoided, the highly visible person is still much better off than his or her invisible counterpart. Career transitions are almost always faster and easier for people who have mastered the art of making themselves visible.

The benefits of visibility are easy to see. It's what every professional wants, to one degree or another. Some want it on a grander scale, but every human craves the validation that comes with truly being seen.

It's not an easy thing to accomplish. Visibility is, in essence, all about how others perceive you, and perception is tricky because it's totally subjective.

Here's the simplest way to break it down:

- Your visibility at work is based on how people *experience* you ... what they see, hear, and feel when you're around.
- This experience, however, is open for interpretation. Two different people may technically see and hear the same thing but have entirely different feelings about it and you.
- How other people interpret their experience is outside of your control. You can, however, *influence* perceptions by intelligently managing the experience they have.

This experience is based on your self-presentation, which includes your physical presence, your actions, your words, and even your thoughts. All of these things combined create the "experience of you." Thankfully, they are all 100% within your control.

Of course, when you're feeling invisible, it seems as if *nothing* is within your control. It's tempting to believe that other people are at fault. They are simply misinterpreting what you're putting out there. It's easier to assume their perceptions of you are wrong; they aren't giving you a fair shot. But this kind of thinking doesn't solve the problem.

The better course of action is to re-evaluate the experience you're creating—to look closely at your self-presentation to better understand what they're seeing (or not seeing). With this level of self-awareness, you can then begin to make adjustments to change the experience.

There may indeed be times when people do genuinely misinterpret how you present yourself. They may create false ideas about who you are and may be unwilling to reshape them, regardless of what you do. Some people just see the world in a twisted way, and you may need to distance yourself from them. But don't jump to this conclusion. By and large, when you're dealing with reasonable people, they're going to have reasonable perceptions that come from reasonable observations.

So, your visibility (or lack of it) is a consequence of your self-presentation and how others interpret it. But simply knowing this is not sufficient to solve the problem.

The prescription that cures the disease of invisibility actually consists of three different ingredients in equal proportion: **reputation, results,** and **relationships.** Self-presentation is the mechanism by which this prescription is created and delivered. The goal is to effectively manage your self-presentation to:

- Build a distinct and credible reputation.
- Achieve measurable and positive results.
- Develop meaningful and strategic relationships.

If you can do this, you will break free of your invisible shackles and reap the rewards of genuine visibility. You will be cured.

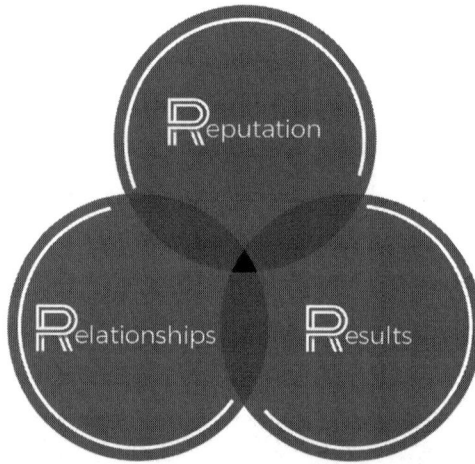

Interestingly, these three ingredients are all interconnected and interdependent, as illustrated in the diagram. Your reputation, for example, impacts your ability to build relationships and achieve results. Each one affects the others, whether positively or negatively. However, you can't focus on one and expect the others to simply fall into place. A strong reputation does not guarantee your ability to build relationships and achieve results; it merely helps, just as a weak reputation hinders your chances of success but doesn't necessarily ensure failure.

The power of the prescription lies in the combination of all three elements. Therefore, you must do the work required to attain each one.

All of the strategies detailed in the following chapters will help you shape your self-presentation to achieve the reputation, results, and relationships you need to enjoy true visibility at work. Each strategy supports all three elements.

However, before you can begin learning and implementing these strategies, there is one more critical concern to address—your mindset.

3

MASTER YOUR MINDSET

As you've already learned, visibility is a reflection of self-presentation, which involves four key elements: your **physical presence**, **actions**, **words**, and yes, even your **thoughts**.

This last one tends to confuse people because thoughts are totally your own. No one knows what you're thinking, except you. Others can only base their perceptions on what they experience—namely, what they see, hear, and feel.

But your thoughts *do* impact how others experience you. They are the seeds from which your actions and words grow. They can also be observed in your physical presence—how you carry yourself, for example, and the "vibe" you bring to a room are physical manifestations of your mindset.

Thoughts are a very important part of self-presentation, and mastering your mindset is a critical first step in raising visibility.

In my experience, people who struggle to achieve visibility

at work commonly have three mental barriers holding them back:

- They don't know how to make themselves visible *in the right way*.
- They don't believe they're truly worthy of being seen.
- They're afraid of visibility—being invisible feels safe, and they worry that being seen will somehow reveal them as a fraud, imposter, or worse.

The first one on this list is easy. This book will give you concrete tools to address the "how" problem. You'll learn strategies to make yourself visible in a way that is authentic, comfortable, and effective. If you're worried about looking arrogant or self-righteous, set that aside for the time being. As you continue reading, you'll learn how to remain humble even as you step into the spotlight.

The two remaining mental blocks on the list are much more challenging to resolve. If you have these beliefs, they are likely having a negative impact on your self-presentation—no matter how hidden you think they might be.

Even recognizing you have these beliefs can be difficult. Often, they disguise themselves as modesty.

I've worked with countless professionals who have very impressive career accomplishments. But when I praise their hard work and acknowledge their achievements, they tell me, "Oh, I've just been lucky," or, "It's really no big deal." They're simply unable to accept positive recognition. It feels so uncomfortable that they instinctively deflect attention away or make self-deprecating statements to downplay their success.

Such behavior is totally counterproductive in the goal of achieving visibility! When you reject praise and acknowledgement, you train people not to give it. Essentially, you're saying, "Look away! Don't notice me! Don't pay attention to me!"

According to psychologists, the vast majority of the population struggles with some degree of "imposter syndrome." This rather ominous-sounding term refers to intense feelings of self-doubt and a fear of being exposed in some way. It's a condition that causes you to believe it's better to be invisible. That way, people won't find out who you *really* are … that you're really just faking your competence, and beneath it all, you have no idea what you're doing. These beliefs are extremely powerful, *even though they are not true.*

Even extraordinarily high-achievers suffer with this. They attribute their successes to luck rather than skill and constantly worry that their most recent achievement will be their last.

These feelings are entirely natural, and if they sound familiar, you're not alone. Right now, as I type these words, I'm plagued by a nagging voice in the back of my mind that tells me I have no business writing a book.

I believe we all have an inner voice of self-sabotage that can hold us back in all areas of life if we're not careful. I call it The Saboteur. This nasty little guy tells us we're not good enough, not smart enough, not *whatever* enough to achieve the things we want. It convinces us that we don't deserve success, or visibility, or love. It assures us that failure is inevitable, so there's no use in trying.

This voice might, at times, sound like a concerned friend, protecting you from the inescapable pain the world is waiting to inflict. But don't be fooled. This is the voice of an enemy.

If you want to be more visible at work and enjoy all of the rewards that come with it, you have to confront The Saboteur. You have to be willing to believe that you *are* worthy of being seen, and that you're not some imposter destined to be exposed. If you don't challenge these negative beliefs, they will continue to leak out in your words, actions, and physical presence, and they will work hard to keep you invisible.

The Saboteur thrives under certain conditions that I'll outline in the coming pages. To challenge it, you must take steps to create different conditions—ones that will be conducive to forming and maintaining a mindset that enhances visibility rather than one that diminishes it.

Compulsive Comparison

As Theodore Roosevelt so aptly said, "Comparison is the thief of joy." But it steals so much more than that. Comparison also robs you of confidence and courage, and The Saboteur fills that empty space with self-doubt.

A certain amount of comparison is to be expected in the workplace. After all, your performance is often measured against that of your peers. Opportunities have to be allocated and dollars distributed. How you stand up to the competition matters if you want to get the biggest possible portion of those things. It's simply not realistic (nor wise) to suggest that you should never pay attention to others or appraise yourself in contrast.

The problem with comparing ourselves to others is that it's an inherently flawed process. We're comparing everything we know about ourselves (including our insecurities, fears, and private quirks) to the very little we know about them. We don't have access to their internal world; all we can measure against is their external world—or rather, the carefully curated picture of it they present to us. In such a matchup, we are always doomed to fall short.

Thus, comparison should be done sparingly and with an understanding of its limitations. Compulsive comparison will only lead you to feel inferior or perpetually "behind." Realize that, no matter what it looks like on the outside, everyone struggles with their own demons and their own version of The Saboteur.

Assess your contributions and those of your peers honestly, and allow others to motivate you in a friendly competition. But don't let their successes diminish your own. Work, and indeed life, aren't zero-sum games. There can be more than one winner. Just because someone already has what you want (or appears to) doesn't mean you can't also have it.

Indulging Perfectionism

Perfectionism provides a plentiful, powerful source of energy for The Saboteur to feed on. As a recovering perfectionist, I know how debilitating this affliction can be.

Here's the problem with perfection: It's a total setup. It's impossible to attain, and The Saboteur knows that. When you aim for perfection, you're destined to fail. And when you do, The Saboteur gets to say, "See? I told you so."

Every time you fall short of perfection, it reinforces the negative beliefs The Saboteur is trying to sell ... and makes them appear more accurate. You start to believe The Saboteur, which only makes him more powerful and more dangerous.

Perfectionism is based in fear. The Saboteur says you have

to be perfect "or else." If you make mistakes, if you let your flaws show, if you don't meet some impossible expectation, you'll suffer the consequences. You'll be discovered for the fraud you are. You'll be subject to criticism, rejection, and ridicule. You'll be *unloved*.

That's really what it comes down to. The little kid inside us all just wants to be loved.

The inability to actually reach perfection leads to a constant sense of dissatisfaction and disappointment. No matter how good you are, you're not perfect. This can eventually lull you into complacency because, after all, if you can't be perfect, why try? And that's exactly what The Saboteur wants.

Most perfectionists trick themselves into believing they just have high standards. But that defense doesn't hold up under scrutiny. High standards are attainable. They're admirable, even! But they are not the same as *perfect* standards.

When you cross the line from high standards into impossible standards, you reach a point of diminishing returns. The time and attention you devote from that point forward are wasted. No one will notice or care about the added work you're putting on yourself.

The drive for perfection is stifling and counterproductive. It is not helping you. Voltaire said, "Perfect is the enemy of good," but it's also the enemy of done. It's a barrier between you and achievement. It's an excuse to procrastinate and avoid risk and devote excessive energy to the wrong things. If you want to gain visibility at work, perfectionism is only making that harder.

You don't have to be perfect to be worthy of acknowledgement, to be respected and valued. You can be your true imperfect self and still be an exceptional performer. You can make mistakes and fall short at times, even in highly visible ways—as long as you also demonstrate a deep capacity to learn, grow, and improve through the experience.

No one should expect you to be perfect, and that includes you.

Dwelling on the Past

The Saboteur only knows the past and is predisposed to only remember the negative. He likes to replay past failures and missteps over and over again, exaggerating them over time, forcing you to relive the embarrassment, shame, guilt, and remorse. He claims he's only motivated by concern. These are cautionary tales! They're reminders that you should never get too confident or call too much attention to yourself. Look what happened last time ...

The problem, of course, is that The Saboteur doesn't know what you're truly capable of. He's a manifestation of fear—a defense mechanism.

Whenever you approach something new, uncomfortable, or even the slightest bit risky, The Saboteur gets loud. He'd be much happier if you'd just stay put and be content right where you are.

But, you're a human being. You have goals, desires, and dreams to work toward, and those things all require a certain amount of risk. You have no idea what the future holds, and neither does The Saboteur. The past is not always a perfect predictor. In fact, the negative things The Saboteur dwells on might actually be the very things that have provided the best lessons for your future success.

Bad past experiences can't be changed ... but they can change you. They can turn you into a stronger person. They can provide wisdom and insight you could never gain elsewhere. The person you were when those things happened is not the same person you are today. You know that, but The Saboteur doesn't.

You have to be smarter than that voice in your head. Dwelling on the past—and allowing it to stifle your future—is not a logical choice. It's emotional. It's driven by instincts that evolved when we were living in caves. Back then, that voice was looking out for our survival. Taking risks could mean the difference between life and death.

These days, we're not facing such extremes, but again, The Saboteur doesn't know that. He thinks he's keeping you safe, but really, he's putting you at greater risk. If you were to listen to him, you'd never step foot outside your comfort zone. You'd be invisible forever—and that would make The Saboteur very happy indeed.

Caring Too Much About Others' Opinions

Visibility is the art of shaping others' opinions. Unfortunately, this topic can really inspire The Saboteur to get vocal. Whenever you're worried about what others think of you, the delicate ego is put in a precarious position.

In the workplace, the opinions of others matter. Research shows that likability is just as important as competence when it comes to earning raises and promotions. That might sound unfair, but it's the nature of the working world.

In high school, I remember being told that I shouldn't care what other people think of me. It was good advice at the time for a self-conscious, awkward teenager. But as an adult who has to function within various diverse communities, it's just not realistic. In fact, psychologists suggest that the only people who don't care at all about what others think of them display antisocial or even sociopathic tendencies. To feel invested in the opinions of others shows that you want to be liked and accepted, which are natural, healthy human desires.

But this investment can go too far. The views of others are important, but they should not dictate your self-worth. Don't define yourself based on how others define you. As previously mentioned, people can be wrong. They can misinterpret your actions and words, attribute inaccurate motives, and judge you without proper evidence.

If someone has a poor opinion of you, it's your responsibility to evaluate the situation honestly. Ask yourself what you have done (or not done) to contribute to the perception and how you might change it.

Also, ask yourself if the perception is *accurate* based on what that person has experienced of you. If it is, you have an opportunity to reform and improve. However, if it's not accurate, don't allow that person's opinion to erode your self-confidence. You are who you are; at times, you may encounter people who don't necessarily appreciate that. You're still valuable and worthy of respect—as long as the behavior you demonstrate is indeed respectable.

You will grow and change throughout your career, as will the opinions of others. If you're proud of who you are, and you're generally well-regarded, don't let The Saboteur exaggerate the minority opinion.

Not all opinions are equal, especially in the workplace. What your boss thinks about you and your work, for example, is far more important than what some random person in another department thinks.

But of course, *everyone* with whom you interact has the ability to impact the trajectory of your career, for better or worse, within your organization and beyond. So, don't disregard someone because you think they don't matter. At the same time, don't lose perspective and don't lose *yourself* in the process.

Isolation

The Saboteur flourishes in isolation. Left unchecked, he grows stronger and his lies grow more believable. In the darkness, things get distorted; it's easier for The Saboteur to disguise himself, and harder for you to distinguish the truth. When his is the only voice, it becomes louder and louder, until it gets impossible to ignore.

But The Saboteur shrinks when held to the light. Under scrutiny, his lies look almost humorous. There's nothing more dangerous to The Saboteur than exposure to the outside world. The more he remains hidden, the more power he has over you.

The most effective way to quiet The Saboteur is to reveal him to people who have your best interests at heart—friends, trusted advisors, mentors, and loved ones. Let him voice his ridiculous perspective and see what they have to say. Even as the words come out of your mouth, they will probably start to sound absurd.

The Saboteur can't fool others. They will see him for exactly what he is, and those who truly want what's best for you will call it out. They'll tell you when your thinking is skewed or when you're acting on fear. They won't let you shy away from doing the hard but necessary things to reach your goals just to keep The Saboteur happy.

Surround yourself with people who lift you up, and don't be

afraid to share your self-doubts. Remember that *everyone* has some degree of negative mental chatter. When you let others in on yours, they will often share their own. You may be surprised to find out how similar the voices are—and how ludicrous the words sound when coming from someone else.

YOU CAN'T TOTALLY ELIMINATE The Saboteur. But you can learn to recognize his voice and confront him when he appears.

A few years ago, I learned a valuable lesson while working with my coach (yes, coaches have coaches; we can't coach ourselves). We were exploring my anxiety about a large corporate training program I was scheduled to deliver the next week. My coach asked me to let The Saboteur out. She wanted to hear all the nasty things he was saying, like ...

"I don't deserve such a large project ... who am I to charge so much money?"

"There's no way my work is worth that."

"They're certain to be disappointed."

"Obviously, I'm going to fail!"

"I'll never get a gig like this again."

... and so on.

When I was done, my coach took a deep breath and said, "Wow. You wouldn't talk to anyone else in the world like that, and you wouldn't let anyone talk to *you* like that either!"

I laughed because I knew she was right. I was a nice person, but I could be a real jerk to myself.

My coach then suggested I talk to myself the way I talk to my best friend—with compassion, encouragement, and love.

This was such a profound moment. I had always been good at supporting others; why couldn't I do that for myself?

Now, whenever The Saboteur shows up, I try to make a conscious shift. I challenge him with another, louder voice—one that believes in who I am and what I'm capable of. I try to let that voice drive my decisions in life.

As you explore the strategies for enhancing your visibility in the following chapters, be prepared for The Saboteur to show up. Putting yourself "out there" in this way can feel risky, and that's a sure-fire way to get his attention. But don't let him go unchallenged. Take steps to actively manage your mindset along the way, so you don't inadvertently sabotage your own success.

Remember: Your thoughts may be silent, but they are not invisible. Your entire self-presentation is a reflection of what's happening in that noisy space between your ears.

4

KNOW AND GROW YOUR VALUE

A few years ago, Janet, a coaching client, came to me in desperate need of job search assistance. She had been trying unsuccessfully to get a promotion at her current company for years and had finally had enough. But, after several months of job searching, Janet had yet to land a new role.

My first order of business was to rewrite her resume, which read like a laundry list of job duties. I spent time diving deep into her experience and put together a brand-new document that highlighted the *value* of her work. Instead of focusing on responsibilities, the new resume cited tangible, measurable results she achieved for her team and organization.

When Janet reviewed my work, she looked slightly confused. Then, a big smile crossed her face.

"I hardly recognize myself," she said. "I wasn't sure it was actually me at first!"

This is a common sentiment from my resume clients, and

it's always a sign that there's more work to do. After all, **how can you expect others to see you clearly when you can't even see yourself clearly?**

If you want to be visible—whether in the workplace or in the job market—it starts with knowing the value you deliver. From there, it's a matter of finding ways to continuously enhance that value.

What Is Value?

The problem is that most people don't understand what value is or how it's created in the workplace. It's about more than duties and responsibilities; it's about the *impact* of those things —the real results you create through your work.

Unfortunately, most people wrongly believe value is tied to any number of irrelevant things. Consequently, they minimize their value, which in turn causes others to do the same.

When I was in my mid-20s, I started a new job as an executive assistant in a wealth management firm. At the time, I really struggled with understanding my value. I looked around at my colleagues and felt inherently "less than."

The vast majority of people working at the firm had more prestigious education than my measly business degree from Sonoma State. They had all kinds of fancy letters after their names (CPA, CFP, CIMA, and so on), and their office walls were filled with framed degrees and certifications.

Some of these people had worked at the organization for many years. How could I ever be valuable as a newbie?

Plus, as an assistant, I knew my work wasn't particularly complicated, especially compared to the sophisticated spreadsheets these folks were working on. I was booking travel, managing the calendar, and organizing meeting materials—not exactly rocket science.

Of course, my understanding of value back then was totally skewed.

My work was indeed valuable because it had the power to affect the organization in very real and tangible ways. The greater the impact, the more valuable I became. It didn't matter whether I had worked there for a year or a decade. It didn't matter where I had gone to school or what I had studied. My value was solely dictated by the impact of my work.

I frequently have to explain this to people when they're considering professional development opportunities. People often believe that obtaining some additional training or certification will solve all their career problems. Once they have those special letters after their name or that fancy credential on their wall, they assume they will automatically be in a better position to demand more pay or finally win that promotion.

But that's not necessarily true.

Organizations don't care about the education you have— they only care about how you can use it to their benefit. If, by obtaining that additional training, you will be able to deliver measurably greater impact, it might be a worthwhile investment. But don't expect to earn the rewards until you can show evidence of that additional impact.

Education itself means little. It helps the organization identify those people who might be capable of delivering greater value, but it delivers no value on its own.

The same can be said for tenure and experience. Sure, once you know the inner workings of your company and field, you should be capable of delivering greater value. But it doesn't automatically make you a more valuable employee. It's all about what you *do* with that knowledge and what you're able to achieve.

You're also not automatically more valuable because you work more hours than anyone else or because you're busier. We've all known people who proudly stay late each night when, if they had just used their time wisely during the day, they could have left on time. Likewise, we've all seen someone who fills their to-do list with meaningless tasks just to be known as that perpetually "overloaded" person who does oh-so much.

Value is not related to any of these things. If you want to understand your true value in the workplace, you have to look at your results above all else. How is your work *impacting* the organization?

Identifying Your Value

This all might sound pretty straightforward in theory, but these concepts can still be hard to apply to your own real-world situation. That's why I've developed a simple methodology to help *any* professional better understand the value he or she delivers in the workplace.

In my time as a coach and a trainer, I've done a lot of research on this topic, and I've been refining my own ideas for many years. In that time, I've identified seven clear ways of delivering value at work. I have yet to find something that falls outside of these categories.

The following table defines the seven ways of delivering value and provides a few examples for each.

Value	Examples
Make money	• Initiate new sales of products and services • Develop new client relationships • Support sales and revenue-producing functions • Upsell/cross-sell existing customers
Save money	• Select price-effective vendors or identify new ones • Negotiate purchase contracts • Reduce usage of supplies and other inventory items • Make smart buying decisions
Improve quality of a product or service	• Deliver exceptional customer service • Identify and/or implement improvements for products or services • Find ways to decrease errors in delivery
Improve efficiency with which a product or service is delivered	• Revise a process to remove duplicate or unnecessary steps • Automate a process • Organize work tools to make processing faster • Document procedures to minimize downtime due to employee absence and increase speed of training
Improve effectiveness of the team	• Help train co-workers • Be a "go to" resource in certain areas of expertise • Lead team projects • Be a positive influence on others
Fix an existing problem	• Identify the problem and/or possible solutions • Define a course of action • Implement the solution
Prevent a future problem	• Identify the problem and/or possible preventative measures • Define a course of action • Implement the preventative measure

Identifying the value you deliver is a process of looking at your past accomplishments, as well as your current duties and responsibilities, through this lens to determine the impact of your work.

For example, imagine you worked on a project to identify and implement new accounting software for your organization. The results of that one project could potentially create positive outcomes in all seven categories. The new software system could increase collection rates, reduce time to payment, reduce errors, improve access to data, and so on.

The goal is to try to gather as much specificity as possible regarding the type and amount of impact your work produced. How much money did you save? How much did efficiency improve?

This is often the hardest part. Results can take some time to see, and a lot of people fail to follow up on their work to find out exactly what impact it had.

Get into the habit of seeking out this important data and capturing it in written format. Sometimes, the results will be clear—you can cite specific numbers of dollars saved or earned, percentage improvement or reduction, and so on.

However, it is also perfectly acceptable to estimate your results, as long as you have a logical explanation behind your numbers. For example, suppose you created a new, more efficient filing system for managing legal contracts in your department. Measuring efficiency can be difficult, but an approximation works just fine. Maybe it took, on average, about one hour to locate a contract using the prior system. Using yours, it takes only about 15 minutes. You've just reduced retrieval time by 75%!

Still, there are times when capturing numbers of any sort

will be impossible. In such cases, you can always use subjective evaluation. For example, suppose you provided mentorship for new team members. While citing numeric results might be hard, you can always identify your own observations regarding the impact of your work. You could say your mentorship helped the new team members assimilate quickly and improved overall team cohesion (these are things that improve efficiency and effectiveness).

You can take any aspect of your job—any task, no matter how small and seemingly insignificant—and identify the value based on these seven categories.

For example, as an executive assistant, my least favorite task was filing paperwork. (Quite honestly, it's still my least favorite task to this day.) I remember feeling like it was such a pointless, unimportant thing to waste my time on, and yet, I had to do it all the time.

When I finally started to understand my value, I looked at this task with a fresh perspective. Because of my time and energy spent filing paperwork:

- Items were quickly and easily accessible for future reference.
- Confidential information was handled properly and didn't fall into the wrong hands.
- Important documents weren't misplaced.

Suddenly, this "pointless" task had value! I was improving efficiency and preventing future problems each time I did it.

Everything you do at work should provide some kind of value. If it doesn't, you need to re-evaluate why you're doing it.

When you're trying to increase your visibility, it's helps to first know that you're delivering real value. With this level of clarity, you have tangible proof that you are a positive contributor. This will influence how you think about yourself and your work, and it will come out in how you speak about it to others. When you know that what you're doing is important and creating a genuine impact, you naturally attract more visibility.

Growing Your Value

Every task for which you are responsible at work is designed to achieve specific, valuable outcomes for the organization. How you do these tasks influences the amount of value the organization receives—and thus, the level of value you're contributing.

If you choose to complete a task as prescribed, you are sufficiently meeting expectations and delivering ordinary value. There's nothing wrong with this. However, it amounts to merely satisfactory workplace performance, which is not usually the kind of work that makes you stand out or get noticed in a positive way.

Alternatively, you can choose to complete the task in a way that enhances the outcome. In doing so, you exceed expectations and deliver *extraordinary* value. Unsurprisingly, this amounts to outstanding workplace performance, which is far more likely to enhance your visibility.

Take, for example, an administrative professional who is responsible for purchasing office supplies. This person could simply follow the standard procedure, place orders for items requested from approved vendors, and ensure the purchased products are received. This is valuable, but not extraordinarily so.

That same admin could add value to the task by doing any number of things, such as:

- Researching vendors to find more competitive pricing and making informed recommendations to decision-makers.
- Aggressively negotiating with existing vendors for better pricing.
- Creating an "office supply sharing" program between departments so inventory doesn't pile up in one area while another is always in need.
- Purchasing in bulk when appropriate to increase savings.
- Strategically purchasing to take advantage of sales, rebates, and discounts.
- Offering tips to help staff members reduce waste of supply inventory, and perhaps starting some kind of competition or reward system to inspire participation.

These value-add tactics aren't defined anywhere in the job description; no one explicitly told the admin to do any of these things. But, using these strategies, this admin could save his or her company thousands of dollars per year.

It stands to reason that an admin who is responsible for creating and implementing these kinds of cost-saving initiatives would stand out from his or her peers. If the admin's actions had a positive impact on the organization's bottom line, he or she is in a much better position to make a compelling case for a raise or even a promotion in the future. This is the kind of outside-the-box thinking that gets noticed and rewarded.

Often, the things that turn ordinary value into extraordinary value are small. They aren't hugely time-consuming or difficult to accomplish. It's just a matter of thinking a little differently.

An easy way to find value-add opportunities in your existing responsibilities is to ask yourself questions.

Questions are a powerful tool for initiating new ways of thinking. When you question what you're doing and how you're doing it, the brain can't help but look for an answer. A 2017 article in *Fast Company* magazine explains the phenomenon like this: "Questions trigger a mental reflex known as 'instinctive elaboration.' When a question is posed, it takes over the brain's thought process. ... (questions) prompt the brain to contemplate a behavior, which increases the probability that it will be acted upon."

So, get curious about your work and how you might add value based on the seven categories identified earlier. Ask yourself questions like:

How can I:

- Make this more profitable?
- Make this less costly?
- Improve quality?
- Improve efficiency?
- Improve effectiveness?
- Fix what isn't working?
- Proactively fix what might stop working soon?

Also, look for value-add opportunities outside of your

existing responsibilities. Your job description is a minimum expectation; its purpose is not to limit you. If you see a way to create a positive impact but it's not specifically "your job," that doesn't mean you can't do it. You may need to obtain approval first, or advocate for the required authority, but even this can be a good thing for your visibility.

For example, a former client of mine, Marie, was an administrative assistant at a large architectural firm. She was deeply committed to her own professional development and strongly felt that the administrative staff at the company needed more training and support. After several years of waiting for something to change, she finally decided to take matters into her own hands. She created a plan to bring the admins together once a month to share best practices and discuss challenges in a solution-focused way. The initiative would be practically free to execute and would require nothing more than a conference room and a commitment from the team.

Marie's proposed plan was quickly accepted, and the response from the administrative team was overwhelmingly positive. Collaboration and communication within the group flourished, admins were engaged, and performance skyrocketed.

Within less than a year, the group gained a solid reputation and leaders started to take notice. On occasion, Marie would ask one of them to join the meeting so they could contribute to the discussion, share company news and offer an "executive perspective" on various issues. She invited subject matter experts throughout the company to present on topics relevant to the group, and before long, she even negotiated a budget to bring in an outside trainer for a full day of education—that's how I came to know Marie and her amazing group of admins.

None of this work was included in Marie's job description. It was beyond the call of duty. In reality, it required only a minimal amount of time and energy, but the payoff was enormous. Not only did Marie create added value in a number of different ways both for the individuals on the admin team *and* her organization as whole, she also became much more visible in the process. This one activity hit on all three of the essential elements: She achieved measurable and positive **results**; built a distinct and credible **reputation**; and developed meaningful, strategic **relationships** along the way.

Knowing the value you deliver and continuously striving to enhance that value are the cornerstones upon which visibility is built. Without this, everything else is hollow. When you're at work, you're there to do a job, and it's valuable, no matter what it is. How you do your job (i.e., the results you're able to achieve through your performance) largely dictates the amount and kind of attention you receive. It's not everything, but it *should* be the most important factor.

∾

A Spirit of Lifelong Learning and Continuous Improvement

One of the most important ways you can demonstrate your value and commitment to enhancing it is to embrace a spirit of lifelong learning and continuous improvement. When it comes to your career, you're either moving forward or moving backward. There's no in-between. When you choose not to grow, you are (by default) choosing to shrink. Complacency is not a real option. As a professional, your learning is never "done." It is my hope that the sheer joy of personal growth will be reason enough for engaging in ongoing professional development activities, but remember that the true value comes when you're be able to use your amazing, ever-expanding intellect to do more, achieve more and contribute more in the workplace.

∽

5

PROMOTE YOUR ACCOMPLISHMENTS

Peor eople unintentionally devalue themselves and their
work in a number of ways, which consequently causes
others to do the same and diminishes visibility. One of
the most common ways people do this is by hiding their
accomplishments or discounting their importance.

Accomplishments are a powerful form of career currency.
They add up and get banked. Over time, they help earn you
rewards like raises and promotions. But they only *become*
currency if people know about them.

All too often, however, professionals shy away from "self-
promotion," because it feels ... icky.

Years ago, I worked with a gentleman (and I use that term
loosely) who had earned his MBA from a world-renowned
business school. While I have the deepest respect for people
who obtain this level of education, my feelings for this
particular individual quickly shifted.

It seemed that, no matter what the conversation, he found a

way to mention the name of his alma mater. We could be talking about web design, electronic filing systems, or what to order for lunch, and he'd inevitably say, "Well, here's how we did it at (insert name of prestigious university)."

I'm keeping the name of the school private to protect its reputation.

Before long, the mere mention of that school garnered extreme eye rolls from everyone on the team.

When most of us think about self-promotion, we think of this guy. You didn't have to work with him, but I'm guessing you've seen something similar. No one wants to be perceived as that arrogant person who constantly brags about all the great things they've done.

To be clear, my colleague had every right to be proud of his accomplishment. I would be too! And he wasn't wrong to want to share his experience in the workplace. But how he did it—and the frequency with which he did—was ultimately his downfall.

There is certainly a right way and a wrong way to approach self-promotion. However, too many people decide not to promote themselves at all instead of learning to do it well.

To make matters worse, many professionals also reject promotion of their accomplishments even when others do it for them. They receive praise or acknowledgement but quickly respond with, "It was nothing," or, "I'm just doing my job."

That little word "just" is especially insidious. It plays a very specific role in the English language, signaling that the listener should immediately devalue whatever comes next. Yet, people use it all the time in relation to themselves and their work. With these four simple letters, they tell the world they want to be invisible.

The words you use (and don't use), along with how and when you use them, are an important part of self-presentation. With the right words, delivered in the right manner, you can raise your visibility in the right way. Similarly, the wrong words, delivered in the wrong manner, may still raise your visibility ... but not in the way you want.

Of course, some people believe that actions speak louder than words, so why bother talking about yourself at all? Shouldn't your work speak for itself?

True, actions are more meaningful than words—that's why Chapter 4 was devoted to the topic of delivering value. That's first and foremost. You have to do things that are worthy of attention.

But that alone does not *draw* attention. It sure would be nice, but it's not realistic. In today's hectic world, if you want people to notice your work, you have to shine a spotlight on it. People are busy. They're pulled in a million different directions at once. Few people are paying attention to what you do (unless it directly impacts them), and those who are will quickly forget. It's your responsibility to help them see what you want them to see.

Being able to comfortably and articulately speak about the value you deliver shows people you know who you are and why you're an important part of the team. It demonstrates self-confidence, which in turn helps others have confidence in you.

How to Talk Yourself Up (Without Feeling Icky)

In my experience, the vast majority of professionals struggle to promote their accomplishments at work, even once they know how important it is. It only comes naturally to a select few—

and a portion of those people do it poorly, like my former colleague.

Self-promotion is a skill, and it has to be practiced if you want to get comfortable with it. Ultimately, isn't that the goal? We all want self-promotion to be a comfortable, non-icky experience, not only for ourselves but for the people with whom we are sharing.

I assure you, it is possible.

To build your self-promotion skills, consider the following six questions before sharing your accomplishments:

1. WHAT are you sharing?

Not everything you do is worthy of promotion. No one wants to hear you broadcast the fact that you arrived to work on time today. That's a basic expectation. Focus on promoting accomplishments that deliver measurable value to your team and/or organization (as described in Chapter 4). Share what you did and the impact it had. If possible, relate the impact directly to the person with whom you're speaking, letting them know how *your* work has or will positively affect *their* work.

Also, be sure you are only taking credit for accomplishments that are truly yours to own. Don't take personal responsibility for something that was really a team effort. You can highlight *your contribution*, but make it clear that others were involved too. (We'll discuss this in depth in Chapter 9.)

2. WHEN are you sharing it?

When promoting your work, use your discretion with regards to timing and frequency. The problem with my arrogant co-worker was that he referred to his MBA and alma mater almost compulsively, no matter what the discussion, and each time, he seemed to go on and on.

I like to think about this in marketing terms. There's good advertising and bad advertising, right? Good advertising is well-timed and informative; it helps you make educated buying decisions. It tells you everything you need to know and doesn't waste your time with gimmicks. Bad advertising is repetitive and annoying. It's that stupid commercial that's always interrupting your favorite show—the one that makes you want to throw something and never buy whatever it is they're selling.

When it comes to self-promotion, you need to do it often enough to be remembered, but not so often that people run away when they see you. It needs to enhance the conversation, not derail it. Plus, you always want to keep it brief. This isn't a 30-minute infomercial; it's a quick 30-second commercial.

3. WHERE are you sharing it?

There are certain settings where self-promotion is not only accepted, it's expected—during a performance review, for example, or in a job interview.

However, you have more opportunities for self-promotion than you think. Far too many professionals fill their everyday interactions and casual conversations with meaningless, unmemorable chatter, which often amounts to wasted opportunities.

Imagine you arrive at work and head to the elevator. But before the doors close, your boss's boss steps on and joins you for the ride up to the 10th floor. He looks over at you and politely asks, "So ... what have you been up to?"

The average professional would probably say something like this: "Oh, you know. Same old, same old," or something equally cliché and uninformative.

What are the chances that your boss's boss would ever remember you after a conversation like that?

You don't want to be like the average professional; you want to be exceptional. Whenever someone asks you what you've been up to, share a recent accomplishment. They are literally inviting you to! Whether you're riding in the elevator, grabbing coffee in the breakroom or passing in the halls, if someone asks about you and your work in a way that suggests they want a *real* answer, provide it. Keep it brief, but don't squander the opportunity.

4. WHO are you sharing it with?

Your workplace superiors are the most important people with whom to share your accomplishments. They're the ones who will make important decisions affecting your career, and you want them to have as much information to work with as possible.

But they aren't the only ones to talk to. In fact, everyone you interact with in a professional capacity represents an opportunity for self-promotion. You never know where people will end up or how careers will progress. A co-worker today might be your boss tomorrow. A colleague in another department might get a job at your dream organization. An acquaintance from your networking group might start her own company and need to hire someone with your exact skillset.

All of these people could be in positions to greatly impact your career in the future—but only if they have a favorable impression of who you are and what you contribute. If you've never shared that with them, you'll blend in with the rest of the crowd.

While you have the opportunity to self-promote to anyone, you still need to be emotionally intelligent in your interactions. Be receptive to non-verbal cues (like eye-contact and body language) that will tell you whether someone is genuinely interested in what you're sharing. If they aren't, don't force it. The timing may be wrong or they may simply not care to get to know you. That's fine!

Also, remember your manners; do not engage in a one-way conversation about yourself. If you want others to know about you, show interest in knowing about them as well.

5. WHY are you sharing it?

Motivation has a way of showing itself. If your purpose in promoting your accomplishments is to make yourself feel superior or make others feel less valuable in comparison, people will see it and feel it. You will come off as condescending and conceited.

Before you share your accomplishments with others, check your motives. Are you doing it to help others understand who you are and how you're contributing? Are you doing it to authentically raise visibility for the truly valuable work you are doing? Or are you just trying to boost your ego and show off a bit?

When you have the right intentions, you're more likely to achieve the right outcomes.

6. HOW are you sharing it?

The final point for consideration is how you share your accomplishments. Experts agree that meaning is derived from a combination of three different communication components: the words you use, your tone of voice, and your body language. Surprisingly, the words themselves are the least important. People can pick up on all kinds of deeper meaning by listening to how you say the words and watching your physical cues.

In my experience, people will usually follow your lead. If you share your accomplishments in a way that says, "I'm only doing this because I'm supposed to. I'm sure you don't really care," that's exactly how people will feel. Likewise, if you speak about your accomplishments with true enthusiasm and joy, they will feel it too. Emotions are contagious; listening to someone who is excited about their work can be invigorating.

Back in my mid-20s, I worked for a startup tech company. Our chief technology officer, Todd, had an incredible passion for the organization and the product his team was building. When he was really fired up, I'd walk by his office and he'd whisper, "Chrissy, you have to come here and see what we're working on. This is so cool."

Todd loved his work so much, he couldn't contain his excitement. He was like a mad scientist, smiling from ear to ear and gesturing wildly as he pointed at things on his computer screen. Much of the time, I had no idea what he was talking about, but it got me jazzed nonetheless; I knew this technical functionality was essential to our company's success. Watching him speak so earnestly about his work, I couldn't help but feel excited too.

While I'm sure he didn't realize it, the CTO demonstrated really smart self-promotion. Not only did he get me pumped about his work, but I went and shared it with others. "You wouldn't believe all the cool stuff Todd is doing," I'd say.

I became a walking, talking billboard advertising Todd's accomplishments.

This is the power of emotion. You can really get people invested in you and your work by helping them *feel* something positive—and that usually happens through tone of voice and body language. These things are reflections of your mindset. How you feel inside impacts how you look and sound on the outside.

Therefore, the most important tool at your disposal when sharing your accomplishments is to manage your thinking. Remember that your work is indeed valuable, and it's worthy of being shared. Talking to others about what you do, in a concise and engaging way, is not a burden to them. It's a professional conversation that is relevant in your shared professional world. It's what people do, and it's not the same as "bragging" when you do it right.

Capture Accomplishments

In training sessions, I'll often ask participants to share a recent accomplishment. Inevitably, I'm met with blank stares and silence.

Recently, a young man in one of my classes responded to my inquiry by saying, "I'm sure I've had some accomplishments

... but I'm drawing a total blank." Everyone around the room nodded in agreement.

This is a common problem that is easily resolved. Most of us expect to simply remember our accomplishments— especially the big, important ones. But relying on your memory is not a sound strategy. It is particularly prone to fail in moments of pressure, when you're put on the spot in a training class, for example, or when you're faced with a rare opportunity to discuss your work with a key leader in the company. Without a little forethought, you'll likely go blank in these moments, and that could be a real setback in your quest for visibility.

You can avoid this by simply documenting your accomplishments on a monthly basis. When you take just a little time to commit them to paper in the structured way I'm going to show you, several things happen:

- First, you'll capture the details in a tangible way and be able to reference the document in the future to sharpen your fuzzy memory.
- Second, the structured approach will force you to really think through all aspects of the accomplishment, which helps reinforce the value of it.
- Finally, by engaging in this practice regularly, your accomplishments will always be top-of-mind, which means you'll be less inclined to go blank in those high-pressure moments.

The structured approach I recommend is called the S.O.A.R. method, which is borrowed from the world of behavioral interviewing. This interview style typically poses questions that start with, "Tell me about a time when ..." The goal is to get the candidate to tell stories about past situations that demonstrate the required skills for the job. The S.O.A.R. method is a powerful way for interviewees to frame their responses.

Consider this strategy a double-whammy: you're learning how to effectively document your accomplishments and you're also practicing for future job interviews. It's a win-win.

Here's a simple overview of the S.O.A.R. method:

S = Situation: What were you trying to achieve and why?

O = Obstacle: What challenges were you facing?

A = Action: What did you do to overcome the challenge and achieve what was needed?

R = Result: What was the outcome and how did it positively impact the team and/or organization?

By identifying all four elements, you'll sufficiently capture the details of the accomplishment. The following table provides a few examples to help illustrate the process:

Situation	Obstacle	Action	Result
I was tasked with renegotiating the lease on our company printer.	The current lease had several unfavorable and costly provisions, that the vendor did not appear willing to change.	I gathered competitive bids and met in-person with the vendor to discuss options.	The vendor agreed to remove half of the unfavorable provisions and adjusted the remaining ones to better meet our needs. This will save the organization approximately $15K over the next year.
Due to the recent merger, our department had to transfer all of our files to a new computer system.	The file transfer was very time consuming and business was at a standstill until it was done. Because of that, we had a very aggressive timeline for completion.	I created a process that streamlined the file transfer, and I stayed late every night for a week to train the team how to use it.	Because of my process, we were able to complete the file transfer ahead of schedule by 5 days, saving the company thousands of dollars in lost productivity.
Our filing system for client contracts was so disorganized, it took hours to find what we were looking for. So, I initiated a project to completely overhaul it.	The files were overflowing with contracts from decades ago and there was really no logical structure at all.	I spent three months purging files, scanning documents that could be stored electronically, and developing a color-coded system for the remaining paper files.	Because of my work, we are now able to find the exact contract we need in a matter of seconds, which saves the team many hours of frustration each week.

Note: While the table doesn't show it, you'll also want to include the date of the accomplishment.

Remember: This methodology is being used to capture your accomplishments; you won't necessarily share *all* of this information with everyone. As mentioned previously, this can be a useful tool for answering questions in a job interview, and you may even share all four components during a performance review. But in almost every other setting, you'll only share the most important details, which are the action and/or the result. Your goal is to be brief, so start there, and if the person you're talking to wants to know more, you can then share the situation and obstacle to provide more context.

For example, suppose you're back in that elevator with your boss's boss and he makes the same inquiry: "What have you been up to?"

This time, with your accomplishments fresh in your mind, you can quickly respond like this:

"Actually, I just finished a tough renegotiation on the contract for our printer. Looks like we'll be able to save about $15,000 this year!"

Should the boss's boss then lean forward and say, "Oh really? Tell me more," you would be prepared to answer by sharing the rest of the details captured in your documentation. By sharing the most attention-grabbing part of your accomplishment first, you create quick interest. Then, you can go further, if and when it's needed.

Do you think an accomplishment like this would be of interest to your boss's boss? Absolutely! Do you think he might remember you a little more because of this conversation? Undoubtedly! Do you think this short elevator ride would create a favorable impression of who you are and what you do? You bet!

Even though you're focused on sharing short snippets of your accomplishments (at least at first), it's still worthwhile to capture all four components in your documentation. The level of detail is up to you, but it's better to have too much than not enough.

Using this structure as a guide will help you concentrate your self-promotion conversations on your tangible contributions, which reduces the chances of coming off poorly. For example, instead of telling people you're a great project manager (which is a subjective opinion that sounds rather arrogant), you can tell people about the recent project you successfully managed. That way, they can draw the conclusion themselves that you're a great project manager.

Accept Praise Graciously

It's not enough to simply promote your accomplishments; you also must be able to accept the resulting praise you will get. It's totally counterproductive to self-promote if you're just going to reject any acknowledgement you receive. The whole goal is to help people see your value. Their complimentary words confirm that you've succeeded.

I realize that praise can be uncomfortable, particularly when it's given for something we don't consider to be a "big deal." But if others are recognizing our work and showing appreciation for it, it's a big deal to *them*. Their praise is a gift— an offering to express gratitude. When you brush it off or minimize what you've done, you're rejecting their gift. You're saying, "I don't think I'm special, so you shouldn't either."

Learning how to graciously accept accolades is a sign of professional maturity. If this is an area where you struggle, I suggest you take a good, hard look at your behaviors and make some modifications. It's easy. All you have to do when someone praises your work is smile and say two small words: "Thank you." If that person wants to carry on for a bit about how grateful they are, or how pleased they are, or how meaningful your work has been to them, *let them.* Don't balk, don't hem and haw, and don't change the conversation. Just listen.

That's all you need to do.

To raise your visibility at work, you must become comfortable with speaking positively about yourself and allowing others to do the same. Release your preconceived notions about what it means to self-promote, and look around you. I'm guessing that, in addition to a few folks who do it poorly, you can also find at least a few people who are doing it *well.* I'm betting they're highly visible and easy to spot. They're probably also the same people who are advancing quickly and seem to have a million opportunities. Let them be role models.

Finally, remember that it's nice when others promote your good work, but we can't rely on them to do it for us. Sure, we all want to find that person who will become a walking, talking billboard for us; with some effort, I'm sure you can create raving fans like that. But, as with most things related to visibility, it's our responsibility first and foremost.

Be your *own* raving fan, and others will follow.

6

DEMONSTRATE EXECUTIVE PRESENCE

A s you learned previously, visibility is a matter of achieving the three R's: reputation, results, and relationships. This is done through self-presentation, which is a mixture of physical presence, actions, words, and thoughts.

Physical presence is a critical, though often misunderstood and underestimated, part of building a distinct and credible reputation. Beyond that, it also plays a big role in helping you develop meaningful and strategic relationships, which contribute to your ability to achieve measurable and positive results.

However, presence can be a difficult thing to define. How do you know if you have the right presence? And if you need to make changes, what exactly does that entail?

Presence is an external demonstration of who you are. I believe it is actually a combination of three different elements:

- Your outward appearance
- How you carry yourself
- The overall vibe people get when they interact with you

Clearly, presence is an individual thing. What you choose to present to the world is totally up to you. However, if your goal is to raise your visibility in the workplace, I recommend that you attempt to demonstrate "executive presence," which I will explain in the coming pages. It can still be your own unique brand of executive presence, but nonetheless, you should always uphold some basic standards.

When I discuss this topic in my coaching and training sessions, it frequently sparks resistance.

"Why can't I just be myself?" people ask. "Am I really expected to wear some kind of mask at work?"

If you're experiencing similar resistance, allow me to share my perspective: The workplace is a unique environment. There are certain social norms and expectations that exist *only* in the workplace. If you don't follow these unspoken "rules," you're creating a distraction that pulls attention away from all the great work you're doing. By following a few simple guidelines, you can help others to truly see the best in you. They aren't preoccupied by the packaging—in fact, the packaging works to enhance the perception of what they're seeing.

If this feels like you're being asked to wear a mask, yes, in some ways that's true. But there's nothing wrong with that! You likely already wear a mask, of one kind or another, at work. The way you present yourself at home with your family is probably different. There, you can be 100% yourself—good, bad, and ugly. But at work, you want people to see your *best* self, not necessarily your *entire* self.

Demonstrating executive presence helps you do just that. When you master this skill, you're able to exude an air of unwavering professionalism. As a result, people view everything you do through a more favorable lens. Their perceptions are tainted (in a positive way); they give you the benefit of *presumed competence.*

After I graduated from college, I worked at a bank where one staff member, Abe, really understood this concept. Abe was a teller who took his job very seriously. While most tellers wore business casual attire, Abe always wore a suit. He was well-spoken and friendly. He had a composed demeanor, a firm handshake, and a self-assured stride.

Every day, customers approached Abe for help, thinking he was the manager. Even when he tried to direct them to the *real* manager, they insisted on working with Abe. His executive presence gave them an automatic sense of confidence in his abilities. They felt they were in good hands, simply because Abe looked the part.

You can probably imagine how things played out for Abe. His career flourished ... *quickly*. Beneath the polished exterior, Abe was also competent, though I wouldn't say exceptionally so. The true secret sauce of Abe's success was that intangible aura of professionalism surrounding him.

Some people, like Abe, are fortunate. They seem to have an innate talent for building and maintaining an executive presence. Thankfully, for the rest of us, this is also a learnable skill. All you need is clear intention and a bit of practice.

Defining Executive Presence

Think about an executive you've worked with or for, presently or in the past. I know there are a lot of less-than-ideal executives out there, but focus on someone you really respected —a person who truly embodies what it means to be an executive in the best way possible.

Now that you have that person in mind, make a list of traits that describe him or her. Consider the three elements of presence outlined previously: their appearance, how they carry themselves, and the overall vibe you (and others) get when interacting with them.

It's no coincidence that most people who do this exercise cite the same descriptors: "confident," "commanding," and "composed," to name a few. The world's most successful, admired executives all have a similar way about them. That's not to say that they all look identical or they all have the exact same way of interacting. Certainly, there are individual differences and there will always be some outliers. But, by and large, successful people at the executive level demonstrate a set of comparable characteristics—and these are the things that create executive presence.

Develop an Executive Appearance

No matter how unfair it may seem, we all make judgements based on outward appearances—even if we rationally know those judgements could be wrong. After all, your mother probably taught you not to judge a book by its cover. Most of us learned the same thing, and yet, watch what people do as they walk around the bookstore. They're instinctively drawn to certain covers, just as they naturally steer clear of others. The same thing happens in the workplace. We're drawn to some people and away from others at first sight.

Maintaining an executive appearance helps you draw people in, or at the very least, it prevents you from inadvertently pushing them away. Within the first moments of seeing you, people are already starting to form judgements; your appearance can either help to create an immediate favorable impression or an immediate unfavorable one.

Let's consider a rather obvious example: Imagine you're a manager who's looking to hire a new person for your team. On interview day, two candidates arrive at the same time and sit in the lobby. When you walk in to greet them, you're met with two very different individuals. One is in jeans and a T-shirt; his face is unshaven and his shaggy hair looks like it hasn't been washed in days. The other is dressed in a business suit—nothing fancy, but very professional. He sports a clean shave, a tidy haircut, a nice briefcase, and a big smile.

If you're like any rational business person, you'll automatically favor the second candidate, simply based on appearance. The first individual might be a great worker, and he might indeed be better than the other guy. But his appearance is so distracting, so far out of sync with the normal expectation, you won't likely care to find out. After all, if you can't even trust him to show up to the interview looking presentable, how would you ever be able to trust him with the big stuff?

Having an executive appearance doesn't mean you have to wear expensive clothing or have any one particular "look." It's not about meeting some pre-defined standard of beauty. You don't need a certain hair color or a certain size waist. You just need to look like a professional. Doing so demonstrates that you care about maintaining the standards of the business world.

As arbitrary as they may seem to some, these basic principles serve a purpose. When people look respectable, they tend to engage in respectable behaviors and demonstrate respect toward others. It's well-documented that your outward appearance has a dramatic impact on your internal sense of self, your choices, and ultimately, your external actions. When you look like a professional, you'll naturally feel more like one and perform like one.

A lot goes into creating your appearance, including wardrobe, accessories, hairstyle, and overall personal hygiene. Once again, there is no single "right" look for which you're aiming. I typically follow two cardinal rules with regards to appearance, and I encourage others to do the same:

1. Create an outward appearance that positions you for the job you *want*, not the job you have.
2. Create an outward appearance that helps you feel confident on the inside.

Your choices are going to depend on a number of things, including who you are as an individual, the environment and culture of your organization, and your professional ambitions.

Every person should hone his or her own personal style as a professional. This can take a long time for some; it's often an exploration process to determine what feels right. Early in my career, I tried to be the "pantsuit" kind of professional woman. I worked mainly in the financial services world, and that was pretty standard. My wardrobe was all black and white, and I rarely wore jewelry. I also didn't pay much attention to my makeup, nails, or hair. My primary concern was keeping the morning get-ready process fast and easy.

At some point, it struck me that these choices weren't an accurate reflection of me, as a person, and they weren't doing me any favors in the visibility department. I didn't feel especially good when I got ready for work ... and I wanted to change that.

I started branching out slowly, and I'll admit: I made a few mistakes along the way. But these days, I know what works best for me. I love to wear a nice, tailored dress, usually in a bright color like royal blue, and a dark blazer. I have a set of classic, beautiful jewelry that I always wear, along with a few necklaces and bracelets I can pick from based on my mood. In terms of shoes, I occasionally get fancy, but as I age, I tend to prefer a more basic look and comfortable feel.

I've also taken the time to truly learn how to apply makeup, do my nails, and wrangle my naturally graying, frizzy hair into a condition that keeps me feeling confident.

If you're a man reading this, perhaps you can now better appreciate what we women go through! While you have fewer concerns, the same principles apply. You might have to try a few different things—switch from traditional ties to bow ties, for example, or try a funky pair of glasses. You might have to devote some time to the process of finding your signature professional "look."

Your workspace is, in a way, an extension of your personal appearance. Odd as it may sound, people make judgements about you based on what they see at your desk and surrounding work area.

As soon as I start to broach this topic in training classes, I inevitably get at least one person who says something like this: "But Chrissy! What difference does it make if my desk looks like a tornado hit it? I can find everything I need, and that's all that should matter."

My response is usually a kinder, gentler version of, "Nope. You're totally wrong."

Once again, it all comes back to perceptions. Your organizational habits (or lack thereof) provide visible clues about who you are and what value you offer. People mentally associate organization with a whole host of other traits, including maturity, discipline, competence, intelligence, focus, and work ethic. This is an example of what psychologists call the "halo effect," where an impression made in one area influences opinions in another.

These associations aren't always true, of course. Organized people aren't *necessarily* any more mature, competent, or intelligent than the next guy. It's not always accurate to say that an organized person is a better worker than a disorganized one, but that's what the subconscious brain tells us. That's the perception.

Imagine the CEO of your company walks past your desk and sees a clean surface, clearly labeled files, a neat stack of paperwork, and an orderly system for managing tasks. In just a few seconds, a perception is born. You look on top of it. You look in control.

Now, imagine the CEO walks past your desk and sees overwhelming piles of paper, Post-it Notes stuck to every surface, Beanie Babies perched on shelves, and coffee cups tucked behind folders hidden behind photos stacked on top of books holding down a big ball of tangled cords.

It's easy to guess what people might think if they saw that. Maybe the CEO would wonder how you ever find anything. Maybe he'd give you the benefit of the doubt that *you* know your system, but he'd probably still wonder how your co-workers find anything when you're out of your office. Maybe he'd wonder if you take your job seriously, or if you'd rather be working at the Beanie Baby factory down the street. Maybe he'd think about doing something else with your office space ...

Okay, that got a bit dramatic there at the end, but you get the idea.

A common argument I hear is this: "Chrissy, if a cluttered desk indicates a cluttered mind, what does an empty desk say?"

No one is saying you have to go to extremes. Just aim for visible order. Remember: You want to look like a professional. The environment over which you are in charge is a direct reflection of you. Plus, research also suggests that an organized workspace improves performance. It's not all about image.

Admittedly, I have seen many executives and even CEOs who can't manage to do this for themselves, but don't let that lull you into complacency. They are still being judged for it! People are just a little quieter in their judgement when it concerns the boss.

Focusing on your outward appearance might seem like a superficial exercise. But it's a critical part of developing executive presence. Just know that it's not *everything*; other factors play equally important roles.

Carry Yourself Like an Executive

Truly embodying an executive presence requires that you go much deeper than your surface-level appearance. You can have all the right gear, from wardrobe to briefcase, but if you don't actually carry yourself like an executive, it's nothing more than a costume. Your demeanor can either help reinforce what you're showing on the outside, or it can overpower it by telling a different story about who you are.

A former client of mine, Claire, experienced this firsthand. If you were to simply see a snapshot of Claire, she would appear to be a true professional. She certainly looked the part. But once that snapshot turned into a moving picture, it was an entirely different show.

Claire was a frazzled mess. She ran around the office wild-eyed, always going a million miles a minute. She constantly complained that she was overloaded and stressed out. In meetings, she chewed her nails and fidgeted, unable to focus on the topic at hand. When anyone asked how Claire was doing, she would always grumble about her overflowing task list and impossible deadlines—she would make it work, of course, but she was just stretched *so* thin!

Claire came to me when she needed help advancing her career. After three failed attempts at earning a promotion, she was finally willing to look at her part in the situation.

Claire discovered that she lacked composure—an essential element of executive presence. When the pressure was on, she couldn't manage her emotions. I had to remind her that it's totally normal to feel stressed, anxious, frustrated, and overwhelmed at work sometimes. We all do! But displaying those emotions—and putting them onto others—is totally counterproductive. Nobody wants to hear it, for one thing. After all, they're dealing with their own stuff. But beyond that, it makes people worry that you're incapable of handling your job.

Humans are incredibly perceptive; we can often sense other people's emotions through body language alone. Just watching Claire run around the office, people could probably tell exactly what she was feeling.

In the workplace, this isn't always a good thing. You don't necessarily want people to know how you're *really* feeling—especially if you're full of fear, self-doubt, and worry. Your facial expressions, tone of voice, posture, and physical movements can all provide telltale signs of your internal state. So, you have to be thoughtful about what you say both with your words and your body. You have to show others what you *want* them to see —confidence, poise, and professionalism—even if it's not the total truth.

People are like mirrors; whatever you show them will be reflected back to you, and in the process, it will become magnified and more real. This can work *for* you or *against* you. For example, if you demonstrate uncertainty, people will presume there's a cause. They'll look for reasons to doubt you. They will treat you with uncertainty, which only affirms your feelings and, consequently, makes them grow.

Likewise, if you show people you're calm, cool, and collected under pressure—*even when you don't feel it*—they will reflect back to you a sense of security, a belief that you have it all under control. This will help you believe in yourself, slowly turning that fake confidence you were showing the world into authentic confidence you truly feel inside.

This is commonly referred to as a "self-fulfilling prophecy."

Whether you're walking down the hall, sitting in a meeting,

or giving a presentation, the way you carry yourself speaks volumes about you. The key is to make conscious choices. It's not always wise to show your inner world to the outer world. Sometimes, you have to be more strategic. You have to pretend like you're not stressed by a messy project. You have to act like you're interested in a boring presentation. You have to claim confidence even when you're secretly freaking out inside. These things don't make you inauthentic; they make you professional.

It's like a performance. When you're at work, you're on stage. Having executive presence means you carry yourself like a professional, *consistently*, regardless of your internal state.

It took me a while to understand this. Early in my career, there were many times when I would walk into work and just not want to be there. I wasn't particularly happy with my career at that point (which, in retrospect, is pretty normal for that age). But I was oblivious to this concept of "presence" and the power it had to shape my experience at work.

When I was unhappy, I wouldn't do anything to hide it. I'd shuffle through the office, shoulders slumped, not making eye contact and not smiling. There was no friendly breakroom banter, no pleasantries exchanged in the halls. I probably looked like I had a dark cloud following me around overhead.

But I finally had a realization: The more I indulged my negative feelings, the bigger they grew. Plus, if I had any hope of actually improving my career situation, I knew the dark cloud wouldn't help.

So, I began to act in contrast to my feelings. Instead of showing how frustrated and discouraged I felt, I decided to show others how I *wanted* to feel: enthusiastic, ambitious, and engaged. I smiled more. I stood taller. I showed interest and restraint. In short, I started to act like a professional rather than a sulky teenager.

This simple change in my demeanor had a dramatic effect on my internal state. Soon, it was no longer an act. I truly felt happier with my position and the work I was doing. I was getting positive feedback from the people around me, and that just further reinforced my feelings. Sure, there were still days and certain situations when I had to work harder at it than others. But I began to enjoy stepping into the steady professional demeanor I had crafted.

I'm not suggesting you stifle your feelings completely. I truly believe that feelings provide important messages. My unhappiness with work in the past was real—I was in the wrong field. I wasn't passionate about the work, and I needed to find a career path that better suited me. I had to pay attention to that and take action to resolve those underlying feelings, but it wasn't appropriate to show those feelings publicly. At times, I could discuss them at work in a measured way, behind closed doors with a select few trusted allies. But mostly, I tried to manage the emotional side of things outside of the workplace.

To demonstrate an executive-level demeanor, think about what you want people to see and what you want reflected back to you. Then, be strategic about what you choose to show the world.

Have Executive-Level Interactions

The last component of executive presence has to do with your interactions with others, or more specifically, how you make other people feel when they engage with you.

Not too long ago, I had a brief meeting with the CEO of a

sizable credit union. Now, I sit with top-level executives on a fairly regular basis, but that doesn't make it any less nerve-wracking. I know their time is precious, and no matter how prepared I am, I always worry that they won't find value in our conversation.

However, this particular CEO immediately put me at ease. He was commanding, but also approachable. He had a busy schedule but gave me his full attention for the 15 minutes we had to talk. He showed a genuine interest in what I was saying; he asked insightful questions, listened attentively, and responded thoughtfully to the questions I asked of him. When I left his office, I felt our conversation had been both productive and enjoyable.

I don't have this same experience with every executive. A lot of them just want to talk *at* me, rather than *with* me, and some make me feel like my presence is an imposition. Others like to play the intimidation game; they sit back in silence like they're judging a talent show. These kinds of meetings always leave me feeling awkward and unsettled.

But the executives who have real presence, like the credit union CEO, are distinctly different. They know how to create an instant connection with almost anyone. They can be authoritative and hospitable at the same time. They foster an atmosphere of mutual respect and camaraderie.

We often see people like this and think they must be master communicators. But it doesn't require exceptional skill; anyone can engage in this kind of executive-level interaction by following the basic principles of professional etiquette.

I realize the word "etiquette" can sound a little stuffy to some. My mother is from the South, so I was raised with a deep appreciation for etiquette. To me, etiquette is not some arbitrary set of rules; it's a way of showing respect for others and helping them feel comfortable. When you demonstrate proper professional etiquette, people are able to focus more on the substance of your interactions because they aren't distracted by feeling uneasy in your presence.

I'm not suggesting that your interactions have to be especially formal or stiff. I simply encourage you to do the small but important things that help set a professional tone, such as:

- Be polite and don't neglect common courtesies.
- Be an easy person to talk to; ask questions, engage in active listening, and participate in the two-way dance of conversation.
- Be tactful, especially when delivering difficult messages.
- Be welcoming, especially when interacting with people for the first time.
- Be attentive; don't multi-task when other people are involved.

This stuff is all pretty simple; don't overcomplicate it. At the same time, don't underestimate its value. When these things are missing, people feel it. They might not know exactly what's off, but the interaction will feel less than satisfying.

To truly have executive presence, you need to learn how to interact with all kinds of people. Demonstrating etiquette is just the foundation. In Chapter 7, we'll go deeper into this topic and look at developing meaningful relationships.

The Importance of Congruence

While the idea of wearing a professional "mask" might feel strange, it's actually very common. Most successful professionals, especially those at higher levels, employ these same strategies. However, I encourage you to develop a professional persona that is at least a partially accurate reflection of your true self. Don't create an *entirely* false identity. If you feel, for whatever reason, that your current role forces you to demonstrate an image that is dramatically different from who you are and who you want to be, you might want to explore other paths. You may be able to find a role or workplace that supports a more authentic alignment between who you are at work and who you are elsewhere.

∾

As you can see, executive presence is about more than simply looking the part. Yes, appearance is one component. But it also requires a deep level of emotional intelligence. Research shows that, as you rise through the ranks of the business world, traditional intelligence and technical expertise become less important for success. Instead, "soft skills" are the true differentiating factor. Well-rounded people who possess intellectual, personal, *and* social competence have an extreme professional advantage.

Look around your workplace and try to identify people who have executive presence—and remember that they may exist at any level. Observe their behaviors and follow their lead. More than likely, they developed their skills by doing the same thing.

As humans, we often learn best by mimicking what we see in others.

Exploring presence can be a fascinating journey of personal discovery. It's about putting your best self out there and creating an image that enhances how people perceive you and your work. Through this process, you get to choose exactly what that image is.

7

DEVELOP MEANINGFUL RELATIONSHIPS

It's been said that career success is more about *who* you know than *what* you know. I disagree. From my perspective, it's about both what you know *and* who you know in relatively equal measure. I would also add that simply knowing people is not really the goal. To truly experience the benefits of a strong professional network, you must build meaningful relationships.

Relationships are at the heart of business, and they are one of the cornerstones for building visibility. *Anyone* in *any* position in the workforce has to interact with people to some degree. The relationships we build—or fail to build—can follow us for a lifetime. They can help us shine bigger and brighter than we ever could on our own, or they can dim our light and keep us hidden in the shadows.

The people with whom you develop strong professional relationships can be incredible advocates for you and your career. They can give you access to new opportunities and help you get where you want to be. Conversely, the people with whom you struggle can prevent you from leveraging new opportunities and even damage your reputation with other people. I've seen bad relationships haunt people for years, and I've seen good ones bear fruit for just as long.

A few months ago, I received an interesting email from one of my blog readers, Sarah. Sarah was discouraged because she had recently been passed over for a promotion. According to Sarah, the boss had "played favorites" and chosen someone he simply liked more. Sarah had more technical qualifications than the other individual, so to her, the boss's selection wasn't fair.

I understand where Sarah's coming from, but I also appreciate the boss's decision. Competence is important, but it's not always the *most* important factor in career advancement. Interpersonal skills can be equally valuable, and sometimes even more so. The boss's choice to promote someone with whom he already has a strong working relationship—even though that person may be technically less qualified—reflects his priorities.

Plus, as biased as it may be, likability is a factor. It's quite possible that the boss's pre-established affinity for the other individual skewed his perspective of each person's fitness for the role. Studies show that, in the workplace, we often judge a person's competence based on our personal feelings toward them. When we like someone, we automatically value their performance more. When we don't like them, we discount their work and minimize their contributions. It's not necessarily logical, but it's how the brain operates.

Thus, the deck was stacked against Sarah from the beginning, but the boss's choice wasn't necessarily wrong. I advised Sarah to accept the situation as an important career lesson, and to focus on building strong professional relationships of her own, both inside and outside the company. Sarah's technical competence would certainly help her career advancement aspirations, but that alone likely wouldn't be enough to take her all the way.

For some, this is a hard reality to face. Shouldn't merit trump everything else?

Think of it this way: Every decision about your career is made by a person. Sometimes, you get to be the person making the decision, but often, those decisions are made by others. Other people decide whether you get the job, or get the raise, or get to work on that big, exciting project. Merit is one consideration. But your relationships with those people (and the people in their sphere of influence) *will* impact their decisions. They might not even consciously realize it, but as humans, they simply can't avoid it.

You can deny it or claim it's unfair, but it doesn't change reality. So why not simply learn to use it to your advantage? After all, your desire for visibility isn't just about enjoying some warm and fuzzy feeling; you want to reap the tangible career rewards. For that, you need people to both see you *and* like you.

Relationship building is similar to the skill of executive presence in that it comes naturally to some but can also be learned. A lot of professionals are surprised to find the process more challenging than they feel it should be—especially if they have a lot of strong personal relationships outside of the workplace. These skills don't always translate from one environment to the other. Workplace relationships have a lot of unique aspects; building, deepening, and maintaining them requires a slightly different approach.

I've found that most people fail to build strong professional relationships for a small handful of reasons, described in this chapter. By addressing these issues head-on, you can create the kind of workplace relationships that not only elevate your visibility, but also help you achieve your career goals.

Defining the Professional Relationship

Too many people fall into the trap of believing that strong professional relationships mean you consider work colleagues to be friends. Some companies even suggest that their employees are like a "family." Unfortunately, these ideas create extremely misguided perceptions and unrealistic expectations. The people you work with and for are not meant to be friends or family. They are professional associates, and that is a fundamentally different relationship.

True friends and close family members are people with whom you can share the intimate, personal details of your life. They love you, and you love them. You can say anything to each other because you know they always have your best interests at heart and vice versa. They are people to have fun with; people who will give without expectation of anything in return.

Professional relationships are not so entirely altruistic; they are unique because they are purposeful. The goal is to collaborate and communicate in a way that improves your ability to get things done together. These relationships are, at their core, built on the premise of mutual benefit. Each person in a professional relationship is working toward a goal. In the strongest relationships, both parties enhance their ability to achieve their goals with the help of the other. It's a win-win.

Workplace friendships are, in my opinion, dangerous

territory. I've seen *many* situations in which workplace friendships create sticky, complicated, and unnecessary interpersonal problems. When people are both friends and co-workers, the social and professional lines can easily become blurred.

Friends have a disagreement outside of work, for example, and inevitably bring that tension with them to the office. Or, on the other end of the spectrum, friends create such a strong personal bond that they have trouble focusing on work during business hours. They can become cliquish and exclude others who aren't a part of the friend group, and before long, the workplace feels like high school.

I've also seen (and personally experienced) cases where superiors and subordinates have deep friendships, and this makes the problem even worse. When you have personal ties to someone, it becomes much harder to respect the organizational hierarchy. Expectations change. As the subordinate, you secretly expect favorable treatment. As the superior, you secretly worry about how to address difficult issues. When all is going well—at work and outside of work—it's no problem. But once an issue surfaces in either arena, it can easily spread into the other.

Additionally, friendships between superiors and subordinates can create problematic perceptions—even when no special treatment is being given. Think back to Sarah, who believed her boss had "played favorites." This might have been because of the depth of the relationship she saw between her boss and the person who got the promotion. Again, it doesn't mean favoritism was necessarily at play. But Sarah's perception may have been warranted.

I advocate for creating *meaningful* professional

relationships, and I would indeed describe such relationships as friendly. But I like to distinguish between "work friends" and "personal friends."

Here's the difference: A work friend is someone you primarily interact with at work. You might hang out together at lunch, grab a cup of coffee, or take a walk in the noon sunshine. You might share a few details about your life that you wouldn't necessarily share with the whole team. You might even grab a cocktail or hit up a kickboxing class together once in a while. But "work friends" have limits that "personal friends" do not.

Personal friends spend significant time together outside of work. They might know one another's families, go on vacation together, or share deeply intimate feelings and beliefs with one another.

I would not encourage these activities with work friends. You already spend a lot of time together at work. Adding a deep level of engagement outside of work can strain the relationship —and this is a relationship that *must* remain functional and productive. Even the best personal relationships are complicated. Why add a new level of complexity to already complicated workplace dynamics?

With work friends, you have to keep perspective. To be blunt, you have to be *adults*. The primary goal is to work together well. A little personal rapport supports that. Too much harms it.

I've had work friends that later, after we went our separate ways in business, became personal friends. We shared more and spent more quality time together. I've also had personal friends that became work friends. As a result, we created a little distance to maintain professionalism. It didn't harm our friendship; but it did change it. We were no longer purely focused on having fun. We had a new primary purpose.

Admittedly, the modern workplace is quite diverse, which means you're expected to create meaningful professional relationships with a wide variety of people. You might not voluntarily *choose* to interact with some of these people in any other circumstance, but in the workplace, you must. Not everyone will become a "work friend." That level of rapport is nice when it happens, but it's usually the exception rather than the rule. More often, work relationships exist in that pleasant gray area between "friend" and "acquaintance."

You can even create meaningful professional relationships with people you don't necessarily like on a personal level, as long as there is mutual respect. I define respect in the workplace as a basic honor and regard for another person's humanity. That means you recognize that *everyone* is inherently valuable, just as they are inherently flawed. We are all human; we're here together on this earth doing the best we can with what we've got.

If we remember this basic truth, we can set aside other feelings and treat everyone with courtesy, consideration, and compassion. We can develop meaningful relationships even with those we might rather not. To me, this is the ultimate sign of a true professional.

Mutual respect is, of course, a two-way road. To build meaningful relationships with others, they must also demonstrate the same respect toward you. If getting respect at work has been challenging for you in the past, I've included some simple recommendations that might help later in this chapter.

At times, you might encounter situations in which respect is missing on one or both sides of the equation. You may have to work with or for people who you simply *can't* respect. You may have to work with or for people who consistently fail to show you respect, no matter what you do.

Should you find yourself in this situation, I encourage you to evaluate it carefully. I find it useful to reflect upon three questions:

- What can I change?
- What can I accept?
- What is unacceptable and therefore *must* be changed?

When it comes to change, remember that you only have control over yourself. You can attempt to gain more respect (by following the recommendations provided in this chapter), but you can't force people to respect you when they don't. Likewise, you can attempt to find respectable aspects of others—no matter how small—but you can't make someone a more respectable person.

In some cases, it may be fine to accept the situation *if it's not particularly consequential.* You're not expected to create meaningful relationships with everyone in the workplace—just the people who matter most (i.e., the ones you work closest with and those you work directly for). I still urge you to treat *everyone* with courtesy, consideration, and compassion. But recognize that there may be people with whom you are simply "going through the motions," and keep your expectations in check.

If, however, a person whom you don't respect (or one who

consistently doesn't respect you) plays a major role in your day-to-day work or has a direct impact on your professional success, you are in a more precarious situation. Creating a meaningful professional relationship in such circumstances will be all but impossible. For most professionals, this would be deemed unacceptable. Consider making a change that removes this obstacle from your path (e.g., request a transfer, find a new job, etc.).

In a workplace where respect is freely given to all by all, I truly believe you can create meaningful professional relationships with *anyone*. Respect is the only requirement, but it is non-negotiable. You may not become "work friends," but, with the help of the other recommendations in this chapter, you will be able to work together in a positive and productive manner, which is the real goal.

～

How to Get More Respect

1. Always demonstrate respectable behaviors and character.
2. Use respectful language when referring to yourself and your contributions.
3. Give respect to others—even if they don't show you the same courtesy.
4. Set appropriate limits; don't allow people to take advantage of you.
5. Tactfully challenge disrespectful words and actions by calling them to attention. You may be able to help others understand how these things are interpreted,

or you will simply show them the behavior will not be ignored.

~

Learn to Adapt

We don't usually get to choose our colleagues; they're simply part of the package when we accept a job. It is highly likely that, in any given work situation, you will be surrounded by people who are different from you—sometimes *very* different.

They'll have different personality traits, workstyles, communication preferences, strengths, weaknesses, education levels, cultural influences, and more. This is beneficial to any organization. A diverse workforce means you get a wider array of perspectives in the mix, which often yields more creativity and innovation, as well as better problem solving and decision making.

But the same diversity that offers so many benefits to the organization also makes your life as an employee a whole lot harder. You have to find ways to communicate and work productively with people you might have very little in common with. Beyond that, if you want to truly succeed, you need to build real relationships with these people, and that requires a certain amount of adaptation.

Adapting is one of the most challenging (and most rewarding) relationship-building skills you can learn. Adapting simply means you flex to "meet people where they are," instead of expecting others to always accommodate you. It means that you accept, and even attempt to appreciate, the differences between you, instead of trying to ignore, minimize, or change them. It means you're willing to occasionally set aside your own needs, wants, opinions, or goals to meet those of others—*for the sake of the relationship.*

Contrary to how it might sound, adapting is not a weak or inauthentic way of behaving; it's actually a demonstration of deep emotional intelligence and personal strength.

I learned the skill of adapting early in my career, while working with a woman named Susan. You see, I am a naturally fast-paced worker; I believe in direct, to-the-point conversation, and I don't waste time with details. For those of you who are familiar with the DISC assessment, I am an off-the-charts "High D" type of person. In more traditional terms, I'm Type A: highly goal-oriented, motivated, and more than a little intense.

On the outside, Susan was my complete opposite in every way. She was slow and methodical, reserved and steady. She had a knack for details and, in my opinion, liked to waste time poring over unimportant minutiae. In DISC terminology, Susan was an extremely "High S" type of person; we could not have been any more dissimilar if we had tried.

I never paid much mind to Susan until we were tapped to work on a project together. As you might guess, things got off to a rocky start. I was ready to jump in headfirst and get to work immediately. But Susan wanted to *plan*, and *discuss options*, and *think about strategy*. I told her we could figure that out along the way, but she wouldn't have it. The more I tried to speed things up, the slower Susan wanted to go. Our first few meetings ended in total frustration for both of us, and meanwhile, the project was dead in the water.

Then, suddenly, it dawned on me: I couldn't change Susan. If I wanted this project to be a success, I was going to have to change myself.

That's when I started adapting. I sacrificed my ego and agreed to follow Susan's lead. Guess what? Our relationship improved and we started making progress! Sure, it was slower than I would have preferred, but we were building a foundation. I began to see that Susan's approach was actually quite smart; I grew to value her systematic way of working.

Over time, we learned to trust one another and developed a mutual appreciation for our differences. Susan even started moving faster and requiring less time for contemplation and discussion. Just as I had adapted to her needs, she had become willing to adapt to mine.

In the end, Susan and I discovered that, beneath the surface, we had a good deal in common. We both cared deeply about the project and performing well. We had different ideas for how to do that, but our goals were ultimately the same.

In a post-project review session with our boss, Susan and I agreed that our opposite personalities had probably made us a better team. While it was difficult to navigate at first, we balanced one another. In addition to our success with the project, we had also developed a strong relationship in the process.

Adapting to others is a sign of emotional maturity. If you can ease interactions and improve relationships by making a few simple adjustments to your own behavior, why wouldn't you? Yes, it can be a little uncomfortable, and it requires a measure of humility. But it works.

If you want to learn to adapt more effectively, start by seeking to understand other people's perspectives. Don't expect everyone to see the world as you do—to want what you want or feel the way you feel. You first have to figure out where someone is before you can meet them there.

Then, be willing to compromise. Don't get so rigidly attached to your own ways of doing things or seeing things that you're not able to bend. Don't hold people to some expectation you have about how they *should* be, or convince yourself that you're "right" and they're "wrong." It's not always that black and white. The workplace is full of complicated social dynamics, and you have to pick your battles wisely.

Beneath everything, we're all in this together. Everyone in the workplace wants the same thing. We all want to do a good job, and we want comfortable, productive relationships that help us reach this goal.

Of course, adapting isn't always the right course of action. Sometimes you need to speak up and vocally advocate for what *you* want. (Don't worry, we'll cover this topic soon enough.)

But don't underestimate the power of adaptation. We have to understand that our colleagues are human just like us, and as such, they have their own unique way of showing up in the world. They have a variety of quirks and personal shortcomings. Just as we adapt to our differences, we also have to learn to forgive minor offenses and let go of petty grievances and irritations. Maybe you'd prefer it if your cubicle mate didn't chomp on celery sticks all day. Maybe you'd rather your boss just take your word on the sales projections instead of always asking to see the data.

In the grand scheme of things, are these issues really such a big deal? Even if they are, you can't just impose your will on others and expect them to change overnight. You need to first demonstrate goodwill; build the relationship so you have some leverage. Often, once you bend to the needs of another, they will bend to meet you in the middle, just as I experienced with Susan.

Adapting means sacrificing your own comfort and your own preferences for those of others. It's a demonstration of selflessness—a gift to those around you.

As with everything I offer, you're welcome to disregard this advice; you can hold tight to your ways and refuse to change for anyone. Some people do, and they are usually labeled "stubborn" and "difficult to work with."

You don't want to be one of those people. Adapting is a simple (though not necessarily *easy*) way to position yourself as a team player and a true professional, capable of working productively with practically anyone.

∾

A Word of Caution

While adapting is an essential skill for building strong professional relationships, it can also be stressful. This is especially true if you are adapting in ways that are far outside of your natural and preferred way of working. The greater the adaptation, the more stress you are likely to feel. If you find that you are continuously adapting in significant ways and it's creating a lot of stress, it may be a sign that you're in the wrong environment. In the right environment, you will still need to adapt, but it shouldn't be overly dramatic or stressful.

∾

Engage in Constructive Conflict

Once again, adapting to the needs and wants of others can certainly ease interactions and improve relationships, but it's not always the best course of action. You don't want to adapt so much that it's like you have no mind of your own. You don't want to let people walk on you or take advantage of you. Sometimes, it's necessary to push back and stand up for what you want and need—even if that's in conflict with someone else.

Conflict isn't always a bad thing. Many of us are trained to see it that way because of bad experiences in the past or simply because it makes us uncomfortable. We usually think of conflict as being destructive; it tears people apart and creates all kinds of negative outcomes, especially in the workplace. Handled poorly, conflict can damage your relationships, decrease productivity, harm your reputation, and cause a great deal of stress for everyone involved.

However, when handled in the appropriate way, conflict can actually be constructive—it can help you build deeper, richer relationships.

The concept of constructive conflict might sound a bit like an oxymoron, but most people have experienced it, particularly with significant others. Maybe you can remember a time when you and your partner had some kind of disagreement. You didn't see eye to eye on something, and before long, the situation escalated into a full-blown argument. Perhaps each of you retreated to separate corners of the house for an hour, but at some point, you came back together and decided to work things out. You talked about the situation calmly and rationally. You each shared your perspectives and tried to understand one another. You looked for common ground and a way to solve the problem that both of you could be happy with.

In that moment, your break*down* turned into a break*through*. When the dust finally settled, you likely understood each other better than ever before. Sure, it was difficult and uncomfortable, but you got through it, and your relationship actually became stronger as a result of it. That is constructive conflict in action.

It also happens frequently in the workplace. If you've ever sat in a meeting where controversial ideas were passionately debated and then an agreement was finally reached, you know how powerful it can be. When people have different opinions and perspectives, and they're free to express them and respectfully challenge those of others, conflict is bound to occur. When everyone handles it in a professional, emotionally intelligent way, this kind of dynamic conversation can result in better decisions and, ultimately, a stronger team.

Engaging in constructive conflict really only requires two things:

First, you need the right attitude. You have to believe that something good can arise out of conflict, and you have to *want* that to happen. You have to care enough about the relationship to make the effort and have enough faith in the relationship to know it can withstand a little heat.

With that as the starting point, you can then approach the situation with a solution-focused mindset. Be open to hearing other people's points of view and even allowing your own to change based on what you hear. Ask people to share their perspectives, *even if you think you already know,* and listen without prejudice.

I like to follow the principle of Hanlon's razor, which

suggests that you shouldn't attribute to malice that which can be adequately explained by ignorance, incompetence, or plain old stupidity. Don't presume to understand people's intent without first giving them the benefit of the doubt.

Second, constructive conflict requires self-control. You have to remain calm and not let your emotions drive the conversation. It's natural to have all kinds of emotions when engaging in difficult conversations like this, but left unchecked, they can taint your perspective and sully your words, which only makes the conversation less productive. If necessary, step away to gather yourself and make sure you're acting intentionally, not impulsively.

Lastly, remember that it's not a personal affront when someone doesn't agree with you. Avoid the urge to protect your ego and make yourself "right" at all costs. You can still persuasively, even powerfully, voice your perspective without making the other person "wrong" in the process. (You'll learn more specific strategies for how to do this in Chapter 8.)

Give First

You've already learned that professional relationships (as we define them here) are purposeful and mutually beneficial, meaning that each party gains something in the process. Still, it's smart to approach your relationships with a "give first" mentality. Instead of thinking about what you can get from others, focus first on what you can do to help and support them in achieving their career goals.

Unfortunately, many people take the exact opposite approach. They don't pay attention to their professional relationships until they need something—like a new job. At that point, traditional wisdom tells them to "leverage their network," so they begin asking for favors.

As you might expect, this strategy doesn't often yield the best results. If you haven't been a supportive, active part of a person's professional world in the recent past, and you're suddenly asking them for an introduction or to pass your resume along to the right person, they're going to feel used. It's pretty easy to ignore a request like that.

By nature, humans are compelled by the Law of Reciprocity, which means if you do something for me, I'm more inclined to do something for you in the future. People want to help people who help them. You shouldn't give with the sole motivation of getting something in return; just realize that generosity works both ways. The more you give, the more you are likely to receive.

Beyond that, embracing a give first mentality makes you more memorable. In today's crowded business world, people are much more inclined to remember someone who has helped them out in some way, no matter how small. Giving to others forges deeper bonds and instills trust. It's no surprise that generous people are often some of the most visible in any workplace.

So, what does this kind of giving look like, practically speaking?

- **Share connections:** Introduce people who might be able to help one another, as well as those who share common interests and goals.
- **Share experiences:** Let others benefit from the knowledge and wisdom you've gained from your unique personal and professional history.

- **Share resources:** Spread the word about articles, conferences, technology, and other useful business tools, strategies, and tips and tricks when you find them.
- **Share opportunities:** Connect people who might be the right fit for new, exciting projects or job openings.

These activities can benefit both your internal network (within your current organization) and your external network (outside your current organization). Through these simple acts, people will begin to see you as a professional ally. And, when the day comes that you need a favor of your own, they will be more than willing to lend a hand.

But remember: It's still your responsibility to ask for help. People can't read your mind. Don't expect your professional contacts to just know exactly what you need when you need it. They'll be happy to help, but they may not offer without a direct request.

Be Consistent

Lastly, allow me to offer one final note regarding the importance of consistency in building relationships.

People are more likely to trust you when they know what to expect—when you show up as the same person day after day. Inconsistency is one of the quickest ways to break trust and damage your relationships.

A few years ago, I was coaching an executive and his assistant, and I saw this firsthand. From our very first meeting, the assistant complained that the executive was impossible to predict (not an uncommon scenario). The boss would show up one morning whistling a happy tune, chatting with everyone he encountered, practically giddy about the day ahead. Then, the next morning, he'd be an absolute ogre. He'd storm through the office, snapping at some people while giving others the silent treatment.

The assistant never knew who would walk through the door, so she was always on edge. She never knew how he would react to things or what he really wanted from her—that seemed to change as often as his mood.

Ultimately, through our coaching, the boss realized his lack of consistency was a problem. I spent time helping him understand the consequences of his unpredictable nature (many of which went beyond the relationship with his assistant) and helping him find tools to create a more measured demeanor.

By bringing the problem to his attention, the boss was able to make some major improvements. He wasn't perfect, of course; no one is. But he became more *conscious*.

I urge you to be conscious of the consistency you show in your interactions with others. Are you showing up as the same person each day? Or are you a Dr. Jekyll and Mr. Hyde? Remember that predictability is comforting. When people know what they can expect, they will be more confident introducing you to others, involving you in their projects, and speaking highly of you when you're not around. They know you will represent them well.

I realize this sounds like a lot—I'm asking you to be both consistent and adaptable. I'm suggesting that you confront conflict while also being generous and respectful to all. I'm encouraging you to build personable, meaningful relationships but cautioning against friendship in the workplace. If you're confused, I wouldn't blame you. Relationships are tricky business. But make no mistake about it: They are an *essential* part of business.

Occasionally, I have met people who truly believe they don't need anyone to be successful professionally. Some even believe their own success *relies* on being a lone wolf—someone who is willing to do anything, even step on others, to get ahead.

These people do succeed sometimes. It's not impossible to make it with a "scorched-earth" mindset. But it sure seems like a miserable way to live.

I believe if you're lonely at the top, you've done something wrong. Success that comes at the expense of others is not worth the price. The relationships we create as we work toward achieving our career goals are truly a gift of the process. They are often as rewarding as the goal itself.

The Visible Remote Worker

Employees who are not physically present in the workplace have an added obstacle when it comes to visibility and building professional relationships. If you're not careful, being out-of-sight can also put you out-of-mind. If you're a remote worker, consider these additional points:

Leverage technology

Strong communication is the key to ensure your physical absence doesn't create barriers in your working relationships. Often, remote employees and their teams rely too heavily on email, IM, and other forms of written communication simply because they are fast and convenient.

Unfortunately, these tools lack conversational context. Without the benefit of body language, facial expressions, and tone of voice, rapport can suffer and misunderstandings can flourish.

Modern video conference technology lets you have face-to-face conversations even from thousands of miles away. You're able to communicate in real-time with colleagues you've perhaps never even met in person. This can be an absolute game-changer when it comes to building interpersonal dynamics remotely. It should be used liberally, especially for conversations that involve any level of nuance.

Email and IM are still perfectly acceptable modes of communication, particularly when your team is spread throughout distant time zones. But don't simply rely on these tools for their ease. Even a good old-fashioned phone call can be more effective (and more efficient).

Technology isn't just a tool for getting things done. It can also support your goal of gaining visibility and deepening relationships, if you use it intelligently.

Be present when possible

Depending on your situation, you may have colleagues in the next city over or on the other side of the world. Obviously, the distance will impact how often you can be physically present with them. Whatever the case may be, you want to take advantage of every opportunity available.

Perhaps you can drive an hour or two to attend a monthly staff meeting, travel to headquarters once a year, or join an offsite retreat on a quarterly basis. It might be a little personally inconvenient for you, but it is a *very* worthwhile investment of time. When it comes to building relationships, nothing is as powerful as in-person contact—even if it's brief and infrequent.

Update your boss frequently

As a remote employee, you don't get the benefit of spontaneous hallway chats or impromptu meetings with your boss. So, take it upon yourself to create opportunities for connecting on a regular basis. Let your boss know what you're working on, what you've accomplished, and what obstacles you need some support to overcome. Remember: When people don't visibly *see* you working day after day, it's a lot easier for them to forget about you or discount your contributions. Don't let that happen.

8

SPEAK UP

Visibility is about more than simply being seen in the physical sense. It's also about being heard. When you speak, people listen. You're able to express your ideas, opinions and perspectives, and even influence others to adopt your point of view on occasion. You're able to vocally advocate for yourself and the things you feel passionately about.

The right kind of visibility also means knowing when to stay quiet, understanding that sometimes, the things you *don't* say can speak volumes.

The relationship between visibility and voice is interesting. With visibility, your voice becomes louder (metaphorically speaking). You're able to command and direct attention. It's like you've been given a microphone; your words carry more weight. At the same time, a powerful voice helps build visibility. When you're able to speak up confidently and substantively, people take note.

Gaining the right kind of visibility requires being vocal in the right way. You have to be thoughtful about what you express, to whom, as well as how you do it and when. Taking the wrong approach can amount to wasted breath, or worse, backfire in creating the wrong kind of visibility.

A few years ago, FedEx released a commercial that beautifully illustrated the complexity of communication. You might remember it.

A group of businessmen are sitting around a conference table brainstorming ideas for cutting costs. One guy, looking very timid and hesitant, speaks up and suggests maybe they could try switching to FedEx to save on shipping costs. His voice, facial expression, and overall mannerism tell us he's not especially confident in his idea. The men gathered around the table shrug, clearly disinterested.

Then, another guy chimes in and very assertively offers the *exact same idea*. Only this guy says it with a confident tone, a confident facial expression, and even a confident hand gesture. Of course, this time, the men around the table love the idea!

The first guy looks astonished and confused. "You just said the same thing I said," he argues, "Only you did ... this ... with your hands."

The commercial became an instant classic because it's just so darn relatable. Who hasn't experienced something similar? I can't tell you how many questions I've received that basically describe this exact scenario. People always want to know why a certain idea, opinion, or perspective they've shared is ignored, while the same one shared by someone else is praised for its brilliance.

My answer is always the same: There's no simple answer.

Sometimes, it's less about the message and more about the

messenger. Some people are very good at making themselves heard—they have not only the skill, but the established reputation that inspires people to listen. Perhaps you simply weren't the right messenger for that particular message.

Sometimes, it's not necessarily the words that matter, so much as the delivery. A valuable message wrapped in the wrong packaging can easily be dismissed. Perhaps you framed your message incorrectly.

And sometimes, it's just bad timing. The idea you presented wasn't right last week, but this week it is. When circumstances change, the same message can be received entirely differently.

There's never a clear answer, but I always encourage self-reflection.

As you explore this topic of speaking up, evaluate your own communication style and habits:

- Do you think about how to deliver important messages (rather than jumping in spontaneously)?
- Do you demonstrate confident body language and tone of voice?
- Do you reflect on experiences to identify better ways of communicating in the future?

These are the fundamental elements of being an effective communicator. If you can't answer "yes" to these questions, start here.

The more you practice the art of speaking up—and the better you get at it—the more visible you will become. The more visible you become, the more readily people will listen.

Be an Active Participant

Not long ago, at my monthly Q&A session, a participant submitted an interesting question. During a recent performance review, her boss had noted her lack of participation in team meetings and encouraged her to get more vocal. She contacted me because, as the team's administrative assistant, she simply didn't feel comfortable chiming in on most topics. She often felt the discussion was outside the realm of her expertise, so what could she possibly offer of value?

This kind of mindset is quite common, especially for those in support roles, but it's very dangerous. In truth, *every* perspective can be valuable. If you've been asked to be a part of a meeting, no matter what your role, there's a reason for it: You have something the group deems important. You don't have to be an expert on the topic to contribute something meaningful. Heck, even just asking a thoughtful question can be a useful spark for discussion.

If you want to gain visibility, you have to be an active participant in everything you do. You can't ever simply blend into the background. At the same time, you want to engage in *purposeful* participation. Don't just speak for the sake of it. Speak because you have something to say. It doesn't have to be especially profound or brilliant; it just needs to add to the conversation in some way. Speaking just to hear your own voice detracts from the conversation.

Pay attention to what's going on around you, whether in a meeting or in your day-to-day operations. Think critically about it. Question what you see, challenge the status quo, and look for better ways of doing things. Allow yourself to have a point of view. You don't necessarily have to convince anyone else to agree with it; just get intellectually curious. You were hired for your brain, so use it.

Yes, it can be difficult to speak up and share your thoughts and ideas, especially in a group setting. But the risk is outweighed by the immense potential reward. The more you do it, the more comfortable it will become—and the more others will come to expect it of you.

Voice Dissent (The Right Way)

There is nothing more valuable than a person who can say something others don't want to hear in such a way that they can actually hear it. People who are willing to say unpopular things, and are able to do so without becoming unpopular themselves, are an asset in any business.

Unfortunately, voicing dissent can be a very lonely, very dangerous road. If done in the wrong way, it can damage your reputation, your relationships, and even your long-term career prospects.

Many years ago, I worked with an individual named Donald who experienced this firsthand. Donald was a very intelligent, highly analytical man whom I truly liked on a personal level. But he was, hands down, the worst teammate I've ever had. The reason? Donald was a "Yeah, But" guy.

Whenever the team was bouncing around ideas, Donald would sigh, and say, "Yeah, but here's the problem with that ..."

Or, "Yeah, but I don't think that's gonna work ..."

Or, "Yeah, but that doesn't sound right ..."

We could always count on Donald to throw a wet blanket on any spark of an idea. It got so bad, people stopped inviting him to meetings, and eventually, he was pushed out of the company entirely.

To be clear, I love a vigorous debate. The more voices the better, I say. Opposing viewpoints help ensure an idea is a good one before real investments are made. Better that someone pokes a hole in your balloon while it's still on the ground than after it's launched.

But it becomes an issue when all you do is poke holes in other people's balloons, and never present a balloon of your own. Like Donald, you can come off as a perpetual downer whose sole contribution is finding problems rather than offering solutions. This kind of behavior doesn't build anything; it only tears down ideas and drains people's energy.

In voicing his skepticism so consistently and in such a negative way, Donald no longer felt like part of the team. He felt like an obstacle we had to overcome.

This situation was utterly preventable. With a few minor adjustments, Donald could have voiced his dissent, even frequently, without becoming the team's problem child. As the great motivational speaker Zig Ziglar said, "You can disagree without being disagreeable." It's all in your approach.

Seek understanding

When faced with an idea or perspective you don't necessarily agree with, your first job is to make sure you really understand what's being presented. Get curious and ask questions to gain clarity ... then *listen*. All too often, people shut down as soon as they hear something that doesn't align with their own point of view; they stop listening and begin formulating a counter-argument. As a result, they miss important information that could change their understanding of what's really being discussed.

I've seen a lot of people engage in lengthy, heated debates only to discover that there's no disagreement—they just misunderstood one another's position. These situations waste valuable time and energy, and make everyone look bad in the process.

Ask for permission first

Once you're certain you understand the other side and you want to voice your dissent, it's often useful to ask for permission first. In doing so, you prepare the other person or people involved for what's to come; you're not just blindsiding them. At the same time, you're allowing them to decide whether they want to hear what you have to say.

For example, you might say something like this:

- "I have a different perspective; would you be open to hearing it?"
- "I see some potential problems with that option; would it makes sense to go through those now?"
- "I'm not sure I agree with that solution; can I explain my thought process?"

Few people will say "no" when presented with these kinds of questions. By agreeing, they will automatically feel more receptive to what you offer because they've knowingly invited you to share your opposing point of view.

Channel your inner diplomat

In the world of international relations, a diplomat's job is to represent and protect their own nation's interests abroad, while at the same time building strong relationships within their host country. It's a delicate role that requires exceptional communication skills.

When voicing dissent, you must learn to be a diplomat—to share a message that others might not want to hear without making anyone feel attacked or defensive.

Diplomats are masters at engaging in constructive conflict, which you learned about in Chapter 7. While it sounds like a contradiction in terms, it is an absolutely essential part of diplomacy.

Embracing the idea that conflict isn't all bad is the first and most important step in this process.

Delivering a difficult or unpopular message, in a way that enhances the conversation rather than destroys it, requires a thoughtful approach. Remember that *what* you communicate is often less important than *how* you communicate it. Your word choice, body language, and tone of voice all influence how your message is received. Strive to demonstrate diplomacy in all aspects of your communication. For example:

- **Use neutral, non-emotional language:** Focus on facts over feelings and avoid placing blame or putting others down in the process of expressing yourself.
- **Maintain open body language:** Show that you are assertive and confident but not aggressive. Don't

close yourself off by folding your arms or avoiding eye contact.

- **Use a measured tone of voice:** This will help you avoid sounding like you're whining, complaining, attacking, or condescending.

Identify alternatives

Years ago, a former manager of mine shared this valuable lesson: "Never bring me a problem without also bringing a solution."

Notice he said "*a* solution," not "*the* solution." My boss was a reasonable man. He didn't expect me to have all the answers, but he did expect me to think about the possibilities. Even if I couldn't offer a perfect solution, he still wanted me to be prepared to discuss my thought process.

I've tried to follow this rule throughout my career, and I share it frequently with the professionals I coach and train. This is a key differentiating factor when voicing dissent. If all you do is focus on the problem, you eventually become part of the problem (like my former colleague, Donald). By also offering solutions, imperfect as they may be, you position yourself as a true team player. You're not simply venting about things you don't like or approve of. You're trying to find a better way.

Think in terms of risk vs. reward

Voicing dissent can be risky. Frankly, the potential reward is not always worth it. Only you can be the judge and decide when it makes sense. However, here are some things to consider:

- What are you trying to achieve by voicing your disagreement or alternative point of view? Is there a positive outcome you want, or do you just want to be heard? If you're motivated by something other than an altruistic desire to expand the conversation and potentially create better results for the team or organization, adding your voice to the mix might not be valuable.

- If you see something happening (or about to happen) that you believe puts the organization or its people at risk (or could in the future), you may feel an ethical obligation to voice your dissent, regardless of the potential fallout. In such cases, how you choose to do it and to whom is very important. You may want to direct your concerns to specific teams who have expertise in dealing with such matters, like your human resources or legal department. This topic is discussed in depth in Chapter 12.

- Be cautious of repeatedly voicing dissent about one thing. At a certain point, if your message is not being accepted, it's time to move on. Continuing to bang the same drum will only make you look stubborn and petulant. Just because you speak up about something doesn't mean anything will necessarily change. You won't always be able to change people's minds or alter the outcome of a situation.

The Power of Pushback

For those who are still skeptical about this idea of voicing dissent, I want to share my experience. This LinkedIn recommendation from my former boss is a glowing testament to the power of pushback.

Stuart Wingate
August 14, 2010, Stuart managed Chrissy directly

I can honestly say Chrissy is one of the most creative, adaptable and genuine people I have ever had the pleasure of managing. No matter what the challenge, she tackles it and owns it. Together we solved many issues and her innovation and willingness to learn and develop new processes made working with her a true joy. She knows when to push back and always has valid reasoning behind her opinions and convinced me to change my mind on multiple occasions based on sound logic. I certainly hope I have the pleasure of working with her again soon!

In his statement, my former boss not only shares his appreciation for the "valid reasoning" and "sound logic" behind my opinions, but acknowledges that this actually convinced him to change his mind on multiple occasions. To me, this is an example of how every workplace should operate. When employees are confident enough to speak their mind in a thoughtful, well-reasoned way, leaders should listen. That won't always guide them to a different conclusion, but when the situation warrants, they should have the humility to be persuaded.

Admittedly, this isn't *always* how the business world works, but in my experience, most people are quite reasonable. When a different point of view is presented, they are willing to hear it out—as long as it's presented in the right way.

Ask for What You Need, Want, and Deserve

In the workplace, you're not always given everything on a silver platter. Often, you have to make direct requests of management. These typically fall into three categories:

- **Things you *need*:** These are required for you to be successful in your role; without them, failure is inevitable. For example, you may need a budget increase on a project you're managing.
- **Things you *want*:** These are not required for you to be successful in your role; without them, failure may still be possible, but it is not inevitable. For example, you may want more consistent communication from your boss regarding policy changes.
- **Things you *deserve*:** These are earned rewards and/or recognitions for your work (like raises, promotions, and other opportunities). They are primarily wants, though at some point, they may actually become needs. For example, you may be prepared to find another job if you don't get the raise you're seeking. Therefore, the raise is required for you to continue successfully in your role. (Just don't frame it so bluntly when you make your case.)

I distinguish these three categories because, even though the approach is basically the same, the degree to which you are willing to push for your request may vary for each. Things you consider true needs clearly warrant a much more assertive, persistent approach. On the other hand, it may not be worth spending too much social capital on things that are just wants.

If the concept of social capital is new to you, here's a quick explanation: In our business relationships, we accumulate an intangible form of currency over time. As we build trust, demonstrate goodwill, and perform well on the job, our capital grows. Each time we ask for a favor from someone, we spend a bit of that capital. If we ask for too many favors from the same person, our capital will eventually run out and they'll no longer be willing to help until the metaphorical account is replenished.

Asking for things you need, want and deserve requires some expenditure of capital—even if it's not really a "favor" in the traditional sense. You're still trading against your established credibility to get something in return. Some requests use only a little capital, while others consume a lot.

Whenever you are making direct requests, stay mindful of the fact that you are using valuable social capital and make sure it's a worthwhile trade. If you feel it could be better used on something else at a later time, it may be wise to save up.

If and when you are ready to make a direct request, use the following steps as a guide.

1. Specifically define what it is that you need, want, or deserve

Vague requests are the easiest ones to ignore or flat-out decline. Just asking for a raise, without being specific about how much you want, is setting yourself up to be disappointed. Just asking for "more" or "less" of anything won't cut it.

So, before you broach this conversation, get very clear on the specifics:

- I need **a $5,000 budget increase** for this project.
- I want **weekly communication with my boss** to discuss policy changes.
- I deserve a **10% raise.**

These bulleted statements do not necessarily represent the

actual words you would say when making your request. Simply saying, "I deserve a 10% raise," would likely come off as entitled and demanding.

I usually suggest that you frame requests as "proposals." For example, "With regards to my pay, I'd like to propose a 10% raise," or, "I'd like to propose that we meet weekly to discuss policy changes."

When discussing needs, however, it is appropriate to be clear that your request is not a proposal—it is a requirement for success. Thus, it would be perfectly fine to say, "I need a $5,000 budget increase for this project."

2. Define why it's needed, wanted, or deserved

Next, you need to be very clear about why you are making this direct request. On a rare few occasions, you may be granted your wish without being asked to justify your reasoning. But it is much more likely that you will need to defend your request with a rational explanation.

- I need the budget increase for this project because the estimated cost for the technology required was inaccurate. The estimate failed to take into account the cost of offsite data storage. We need this to ensure our confidential client information is protected.
- I want weekly communication from my boss regarding policy changes because the sooner I get the information, the sooner I can update our manuals. If I don't hear about changes until weeks or months after they've gone into effect, our people are

working with outdated manuals during that time. Because of the delay in communication, error rates have been going up recently.

- I deserve a 10% raise because, over the past year, I saved the organization $10,000 in toner fees by creating the "Think Twice Before You Print" campaign. This raise would represent only a portion of what the organization has saved and will continue to save moving forward.

You can look back at Chapter 4 (Know and Grow Your Value) and Chapter 5 (Promote Your Accomplishments) for more insight on how to justify your request for a raise, promotion or other reward/recognition.

Additionally, note that the request for a raise has nothing to do with financial need. You should never try to justify a raise by saying, "My car needs to be replaced!" or, "My kid needs braces!" These are not appropriate reasons. You're asking for something you *deserve*. Prove why you deserve it.

3. Provide evidence to support your case

Providing physical evidence that supports your request will help make your case more compelling. The goal is to offer some kind of backup that proves your request is reasonable.

- To support the $5,000 budget increase, you could provide a quote from several offsite data storage companies.
- To support the weekly communication request, you

could provide a report that shows the increasing
error rates caused by the outdated policy manuals.

- To support the 10% raise, you could provide a report
that shows the toner expenses from last year
compared to this year, as well as projected savings
going forward.

Any time you're discussing salary, it's important to conduct
salary research ahead of time. You can find many websites that
provide up-to-date information regarding average and median
salary for people in your area who hold your job title. Usually,
you will find a range that looks like a bell curve, where the
majority of people make the middle amount, and smaller
numbers of people make the amounts extended to each side.

When preparing to ask for a raise, determine where you
believe you should fall on the bell curve, and remember to keep
your request reasonable. Even if you believe you deserve to
move from one far end of the spectrum to the other, it's more
likely to happen with incremental steps.

4. If possible, offer ideas for "how" it might be accomplished

When making a request, you want to make it as easy as possible
for the decision-maker to say "yes." If possible, it's worth your
time to do the hard part for them and provide suggestions for
how it might happen. You don't have to have the perfect answer;
but something is better than nothing. At least they won't have to
start from scratch to figure it out.

Clearly, this isn't always feasible. You might not know how
budgets are allocated all over the organization and where funds

can be pulled from to support your request. But use whatever is at your disposal.

Considering the three examples we've been working with, the second is one for which you can clearly offer suggestions. How do you envision this weekly communication with your boss to happen? Do you suggest a standing meeting on Friday afternoons? Should it take place by phone or in person? Would an email update suffice? The less your boss has to think about logistics, the more likely he or she will agree to your request.

5. Prepare to negotiate

I wish I could tell you that, with the right approach, all of your requests are guaranteed to be accepted. Sadly, that's just not realistic.

All kinds of things may factor into a decision, and many of them are outside your control—some are even outside of your boss's control. However, presenting your case in the strongest way possible, as outlined here, puts you in the best position for success. You may not always get exactly what you ask for, but if you're willing to flex a bit, you may get at least *part* of what you ask for, which is better than nothing!

Don't be afraid to get a little creative too. If your much-deserved raise just isn't in the budget right now, maybe you can negotiate some extra flex time. If your boss isn't able to meet with you weekly, maybe you can meet every other week. Try not to take an all-or-nothing mentality.

∾

Asking Works

According to a 2018 study conducted by PayScale, only 37% of workers have asked for a raise. However, of those who did ask, 70% received a pay increase; 39% scored the amount they requested, while the other 31% received a smaller amount than requested, though they still got *something*. The lesson? Just ask! The worst that can happen is you won't get it. But the odds are in your favor.

∼

ONE COMMON AREA where I see potential for more negotiation is around requests for professional development. People often tell me they want to participate in a training course or attend an industry conference, but their company won't pay for it. Most people give up when they hear that. However, there are so many other options to consider! Maybe your company would be willing to share the cost with you, or perhaps they would agree to give you some added paid days off to attend that conference. A lot of different roads could lead to the same (or similar) destination.

As the saying goes, "The squeaky wheel gets the grease." When you need, want, or deserve something, you have to speak up to make it happen. People can't read your mind. When you're silent, they'll assume the status quo is perfectly acceptable.

The worst that can happen when you make a request is that you'll be told "no." And it *will* happen from time to time. But at least you've made your voice heard. At least you tried. Depending on the situation, you might be able to work with your boss to create a plan for how to get to "yes" in the future.

The subtitle of this book is "How to Stand Out, Get Noticed, and Get What You Want at Work." That last part is tricky because, as the Rolling Stones say, you can't always get what you want. Here's how I think of it: I do believe you can get what you want at work, but not always exactly when you want it. And sometimes, you have to go somewhere different or do something different to get what you want. But as long as what you want is reasonable, there's a way to make it happen.

The strategies discussed in this chapter are not easy. Being a vocal advocate for yourself, sharing your ideas, and expressing unfavorable opinions may not ever feel completely natural. But I encourage you to step up to the challenge. In this uncomfortable territory, you have the power to attract a lot of attention. The thoughtful approach outlined in this chapter will help ensure it's the positive kind.

9

LIFT OTHERS

As you've already learned, building strong professional relationships is a key part of gaining visibility. One way you can do that is by helping to lift others up. When you help the people around you maintain energy and optimism, and provide the support they need to be successful, everyone wins. This is what is meant by the aphorism, "A rising tide lifts all boats."

A former client of mine, Anne, was a true testament to the power of this concept. Anne was a C-suite executive assistant and probably one of the most well-known, well-respected people in her global corporation. However, Anne's high level of visibility wasn't simply due to her role. It was because of her ability to bring out the best in people.

Anne was a warm-hearted, generous person. Regardless of her busy schedule, she always made time to mentor junior-level assistants. Heck, even some high-ranking executives saw Anne as a role model, a confidant, and an enthusiastic supporter.

People regularly came to her for advice; they often entered her office in a state of confusion, frustration, or despair, and left feeling confident and empowered. Because of who Anne was, she enjoyed an incredible amount of influence—far greater than any other assistant in any other organization I've seen.

When Anne was preparing for retirement, she invited me to work with her team to help create a transition plan. There were quite a few tears shed during that process! A year after Anne's departure, I checked in with each of the team members to see how things were going. Without exception, everyone said the same thing: Work-wise, the transition had been smooth. Anne's special projects were all successfully moving forward and her "replacement" was managing well. But no one could really replace Anne. She was still missed desperately throughout the organization—not necessarily for the work she did, but for her presence.

The truth is, people probably relied on Anne a little too much. This can happen when you have someone who is *that* skilled at lifting others. But, as Anne's team learned, sometimes you have to stop relying on someone else to be that person and become that person yourself.

Anne was a pretty unique individual. But anyone can learn to be like her. The strategies provided in this chapter will help you embrace a similar spirit.

Share Credit and Recognize Others

In Chapter 5, you learned the importance of articulating your accomplishments and how to do that in a way that feels comfortable for everyone. A critical part of that process is to ensure that you're only taking credit for your own work, and rightfully sharing credit with others where it's due.

Nothing is more deflating than watching someone else get recognition for your work. If you've ever experienced it, you know the feeling. No one should take credit or allow others to give them credit for work that is not theirs. However, if you want to lift others, it goes beyond that. You also need to actively recognize and help promote the work of others.

For a lot of people, this can feel a little uncomfortable. It's hard enough to get recognition for your own work. And, if you're not someone's manager, is it really your place to tell them they did a good job? Wouldn't that come off as patronizing?

In my experience, everyone likes the feeling of praise, and in today's workplace, there's not enough of it going around. I am a firm believer that *anyone* can offer positive recognition to *anyone*—whether the person is above you, beside you, or below you on the org chart. I'm not talking about some condescending pat-on-the-head-style praise. I'm talking about offering genuine acknowledgement of a job well done.

While it may seem counterintuitive, when you help others feel more visible, you become more visible yourself. Showing appreciation for the work of others demonstrates a number of attention-worthy traits:

- **You show you're a team player:** When you talk about team efforts from a "we" perspective (rather than "I"), you become known as a good person to partner with.
- **You prove your confidence:** Acknowledging the work of others shows that you're not insecure; you're

not afraid of letting someone else have a moment of glory.

- **You demonstrate leadership:** Offering positive feedback is typically seen as the job of leadership. In doing it yourself, you create a reputation for having the qualities of a leader, regardless of your title or aspirations.
- **You become more memorable:** People don't quickly forget those who help them feel a sense of pride and achievement. Even a small acknowledgement can stay with someone for a long time.

This kind of praise can happen both in public and in private. Imagine you're in a meeting and you're asked to report on the status of a project. Let's say Bill in accounting provided some timely data that really helped you make headway on this project over the past week. Why not give Bill a shout-out in front of the group? If everyone has an interest in the status of the project, they'll all certainly appreciate Bill's work.

(To be clear, I'm not suggesting that you turn the spotlight on others as a means of avoiding it yourself. There's enough light to go around.)

You don't have to publicize your acknowledgement to make it valuable to the individual. For example, if someone on your team earns a promotion or receives a special award, congratulate them. Go to their office or give them a call and let them know you're happy for them. Too often, teammates get weird in these moments. They might not actually be jealous, but they act like it. They ignore what's going on and make the person who just achieved something great feel uncomfortable about it. Please don't do that.

Remember that work isn't a zero-sum game. Someone else's success does not diminish your success. In fact, quite the opposite is true. When you are surrounded by successful people, your chances of success tend to increase. That's the rising tide in action.

Dealing With Credit Thieves

While I encourage you to freely share credit with others in the workplace, I realize you may encounter times where credit is stolen from you. I frequently hear this from clients, and when I do, I typically offer two important points for consideration:

First, recognize that managers often receive praise on behalf of their team. A good manager will publicly acknowledge those who made the achievements possible and make sure the praise flows down to the people who deserve it. But they can't necessarily do that with every little thing. I heard an assistant complain that her boss received great compliments on a presentation he gave but didn't tell anyone that she made the slides. This kind of thing happens frequently, especially for people in support roles. It shouldn't be an issue; it's not the same thing as stealing credit. A variety of things likely contributed to the boss's great presentation; the slides may have been one part. But it's not like he claimed to have done them.

Would it be nice if the boss turned around and acknowledged the assistant for her role in helping him give a great presentation? Absolutely. But this kind of oversight isn't the severe slight it might seem.

Some situations are more serious, which brings me to my second point: The most effective way to stop credit thieves in their tracks is to be vocal. No one can steal credit when you've been consistently loud about your work. Refer back to Chapter 5 for tips on how to do it in a way that feels comfortable for everyone. Just remember: When you stay silent, you make it very easy for others to step in and create their own version of events.

Demonstrate an Attractive Attitude

Your attitude has the ability to impact others in dramatic ways. It can help lift them up or it can drag them down.

You may remember the popular *Saturday Night Live* sketch about Debbie Downer. If you haven't ever seen it or if it's been a while, put the book down and go watch a clip on YouTube. Go ahead, I'll wait.

Okay, Debbie Downer is obviously an exaggerated character. But, as with most good comedy, we can all kind of relate. Most of us have known someone who is perpetually negative and pessimistic, and we know how difficult it is to be around them. They are like energy vampires—they suck the life out of every room they enter.

Most people don't enjoy spending time with someone who is a relentless downer. In the workplace, being labeled a "Negative Nancy" or "Bad News Bob" will give you visibility, all right ... but the wrong kind. People will notice you because they'll be steering clear of your path.

On the other hand, the right attitude can really draw people in. There's something almost magnetic about people who have a certain way of looking at the world. It's hard to define exactly, but over the years I've done my best to identify the key traits of what I call an "Attractive Attitude." This is, in my experience, the kind of attitude that makes people not only enjoy your presence, but desire it, and miss it when you're gone. The three elements—**positivity**, **possibility,** and **power**—are described below.

Positivity

This is an undeniably important part of the Attractive Attitude, but I want to be clear: I'm not talking about being relentlessly positive. You don't have to force positivity into every situation. In fact, a persistent drive to put a positive spin on everything can be dangerous. Forced positivity can crowd out important information. It can blind you to the truth of a situation and make you look disconnected from reality.

Plenty of negative things happen in the workplace. People get laid off, clients complain, projects fail. Being positive doesn't mean you're trying to put a bright spin on anything and everything.

Instead, positivity is believing there is a solution to any problem you may face. When challenges arise, and when times are tough, a positive attitude means you truly believe that things can and will get resolved. The solution might not be easy or fun, and it might not feel good for the people involved. But, without a doubt, you know the situation will eventually improve if you do what you need to do.

Possibility

Embracing the element of possibility means believing that anything can happen—even things that might appear on the surface to be impossible. It means understanding that there are always multiple angles to any situation, and there may be things you don't yet know that change your understanding. It's about keeping an open mind and looking for new perspectives that shine new light on the challenges you're facing.

Power

Finally, power means believing *you* have an impact. That your presence, your ideas, your intelligence, your actions, and your words all have the ability to influence a situation positively or negatively. When you embrace your power, you recognize the responsibility of that power. You use your influence to help find and implement solutions rather than dwell in the problem. Power is about believing you can make things happen.

By demonstrating an Attractive Attitude, you will naturally pull people toward you rather than push them away. They will seek your counsel, pursue your participation, and invite your input. They will *want* your involvement. Why? Because your attitude is attractive. Your contributions help elevate the conversation and encourage others to rise to new heights.

Be a Friendly Ear

Most workplaces have a lot going on—high-pressure deadlines, overwhelming workloads, and complicated social dynamics make for a stressful environment. It's enough to make even the most well-balanced individual lose it on occasion.

Studies have shown that having a workplace confidant can be one of the most powerful tools for achieving long-term job satisfaction. When you have someone to whom you can confidentially and productively "vent" about workplace frustrations, you're able to manage those frustrations more effectively.

You can offer support to your colleagues by being that friendly ear. However, it is important that you are thoughtful in how you go about doing it. Otherwise, your "support" can look more like a gossip/complaint/therapy session. When that happens, you're putting yourself in dangerous, messy territory.

The key is to remember that venting has a point of diminishing returns. It's helpful to uninhibitedly express your honest thoughts and feelings, no matter how negative, for a period of time. But it gradually becomes less helpful, and at a certain point, it becomes counterproductive. It no longer feels like a cathartic relief, and instead, it actually starts to increase your stress, anxiety, anger, and other emotions.

Your job, as the supportive confidant, is to listen without judgement *for a short period of time*. Then, help steer the conversation in a more constructive direction.

When someone is venting about work frustrations, don't actively agree with them or egg them on by adding in your own similar frustrations. More than likely, you don't know the whole situation and you probably don't want to get involved by looking like you're taking sides. The more you encourage them, the more heightened their frustrations will become.

Simply listen and be empathetic. In some cases, you can also help them see other perspectives and point out angles they might not be considering. With a little thoughtful conversation, you might be able to help them realize their frustration is misplaced.

Once the initial steam has been let off, help the person identify solutions for moving forward. You don't have to offer solutions yourself; you just want to turn their attention away from the problem and toward a possible resolution. Try asking questions like:

- What do you think you should do now?
- What's the path forward look like?
- What options do you have?
- How does this get resolved?
- How can I help you resolve this?

While you want to be a supportive colleague, you also have to protect yourself and your time. Don't allow someone to absorb endless hours with unproductive venting. You're not a therapist. It's perfectly acceptable to let people know that you're sympathetic, but you're not available to talk.

Train and Mentor Others

One of the greatest gifts you can give a person is to help them develop. By sharing your professional knowledge with a colleague, you are potentially impacting their entire career journey and, in a wider sense, their entire *life* journey.

All too often, I find that professionals like to hoard knowledge. It's just like *Hoarders*—that TV show about people who accumulate so much stuff, they're eventually nearly buried alive by it. At work, people accumulate information and refuse to share it with others, which is just as dangerous in its own way.

People become very territorial in the workplace, especially when it's a competitive one. They don't want anyone else to know what they know or how to do what they do. They think this hoarder mentality will somehow give them more job security; it will make them more important, more necessary, more irreplaceable.

It doesn't work that way. By hoarding your knowledge, you're not protecting yourself. Everyone can see what you're doing. You can't hold your organization or your team hostage by withholding information. Doing so only makes you look insecure.

On the other hand, those who freely share their knowledge and give people the information they need to be successful are seen as true team players and leaders. *These* are the people the organization really needs. *These* are the people everyone wants on their team.

If you and your colleagues all have to work on the same report each week, and you discover a new trick that makes it a much faster task, teach everyone else how to do it too. Why deny them the benefit of that knowledge? What good does it do you to hold on to it?

If that trick saves you 30 minutes and you share it with three colleagues, that's two hours saved each week. Sure, keep it to yourself and you get to the be the fastest. But share it and you get to be that genius who saved the team hours of work each week. They'll be forever grateful, *and* you'll have a great accomplishment to share with your boss.

This isn't just about sharing tips and tricks and how-to's. You also possess a wealth of wisdom gained through your unique professional history. Through mentorship, you can help others leverage your experience and learn from your mistakes. No matter where you are in your career, you have something valuable to offer someone. Even if it's only your second day on the job, you know more than the person who's walking in fresh on their first day. Show them where the bathroom is and help them get a cup of coffee.

The most basic definition of mentorship is simply "guidance offered by a trusted source." It doesn't have to be a formal affair. According to recent studies, fewer than 30% of workplaces offer mentorship programs. If yours does, by all means, get involved. Sign up to be both a mentee and a mentor. But even if your organization doesn't have a program, you can still provide guidance to those who need it.

Providing guidance does not mean that you should try to tell people what to do. The best mentors share their own experiences, offer thoughtful perspectives, ask challenging questions, and ultimately, help people make their own decisions. Be careful about inserting your own opinions too deeply into the conversation. You don't want to give someone direction that backfires. Let them find their own way and support them in getting there.

~

The Two-Way Career Benefits of Mentorship
A 2006 study of a mentorship program inside of Sun
Microsystems found the following:

- 25% of the people mentored earned an increased salary within the study period (compared to just 5% of non-mentored employees).
- People who were mentored were promoted five times more than those not mentored.
- Mentors themselves received promotions six times more often than non-mentors.

Clearly, mentorship has significant career benefits for *both* parties.

∼

WHEN YOU FIRST SAW THE title of this chapter (Lift Others), you may have been worried that I would ask you to become some kind of cheerleader. Hopefully you can now see that pom-poms and chants aren't required. I'm not much of a "rah-rah" kind of person. But I do believe everyone needs support. The workplace can feel very isolating. Heck, in today's high-tech world, life itself can feel isolating. As humans, we need each other.

When we help others, we also help ourselves. This is called "enlightened self-interest." When we support the people around us, we increase our own visibility and increase the chances that they'll support us in the future. It's not a purely selfless act, and that's okay. It's still a generous and kind act that benefits others, even if it also benefits you in the process.

10

TAKE OWNERSHIP

A few years ago, I had lunch with a very successful executive who had just hired a new assistant. During our meal, he told me of a situation that had opened his eyes to an important concept.

The assistant had been in her job for only a few weeks when the executive mentioned, in an off-handed kind of way, that he was thinking about getting the team involved in a charitable activity of some sort that year—something like a fundraiser or a day of service. He didn't quite know; he was just thinking aloud.

A few days later, the assistant handed him a file. Inside, he found a list of charitable organizations in the area, a brief overview of each one's mission, and a list of possible activities for the volunteer team to engage in.

The executive was delighted. He told me that the new assistant really "owned" her position. It wasn't so much about the task or the project. She understood that her job was to help make his life easier and his work more effective —and she felt a deep sense of ownership over that. He didn't have to ask her to do it; she was actively looking for ways to do it.

He told me that the previous assistant was adequate, but in all their years working together, she had never taken that kind of ownership over her work.

This was a profound experience that led the executive to an important conclusion: He wanted a whole team of owners— people who were willing to take 100% responsibility for their own success. He didn't want "employees" who needed "management." He wanted to *lead* motivated, dedicated professionals.

Most business leaders want the same thing, even if they aren't able to articulate it quite so clearly. But it's surprisingly uncommon. Therefore, those who do take an ownership approach in the workplace tend to stand out in a powerful and positive way.

When we talk about taking ownership, we're really talking about a combination of two different ingredients: investment and initiative. People who "own" their work:

- Are deeply invested in the *outcome*; they understand the results they're trying to achieve and are committed to making them happen.
- Take initiative to do what needs to be done; they don't require specific instruction from others.

I explored these topics at great length in my previous book, *The Proactive Professional* (available on Amazon and other major book retailers). So, in this chapter, my goal is to provide a few additional high-level thoughts to support your growth in this area.

~

"Here's the basic rule for taking initiative: **If you know what needs to be done and you know it's something within the scope of your position and capabilities, *do it*.** Don't wait for direction. Don't look for approval. Don't hand it off to someone else. Take Intentional Action. No permission or forgiveness needed. If you're qualified by virtue of your job and your abilities, there's no reason to question yourself."

— The Proactive Professional: How to Stop Playing Catch Up & Start Getting Ahead at Work (and in Life!)

~

Think Like an Entrepreneur

I became a business owner in 2009, and I'm comfortable now admitting that I was woefully ill-prepared. Like many entrepreneurs, I learned mostly through trial and error. I had to figure out how to run a business while also attempting to run one. For the first five years, I did everything myself—marketing, sales, accounting, IT, you name it. I built my own website, did my own taxes, and designed my own brochures, all while providing coaching and training services.

These days, I still do a lot on my own, but I'm fortunate enough to have some help in a few key areas. I'm also incredibly grateful for everything I learned in those early years. No one knows my business better than I do. No one cares about it more than I do. I'm not afraid to roll up my sleeves and do whatever has to be done to make sure my business is a success.

According to the U.S. Small Business Administration, the failure rate for American small businesses is 30% within the first year, 50% in the first five years, and 66% in the first 10. I've beaten the odds time and time again, so I must be doing something right.

I believe that every professional, regardless of role, can benefit from learning to think like an entrepreneur. At the most fundamental level, business owners understand that *they* are responsible for the success or failure of their enterprise. You'll never hear them say, "That's not my job," because their job is to make the business successful. They'll do whatever is required to reach that goal, even if it means learning a brand-new skill, or doing the grunt work, or putting in crazy amounts of overtime. They have nearly inexhaustible enthusiasm and unwavering dedication to the mission.

As an employee, you don't have the same pressures as a business owner, nor do you have the same freedom to do anything and everything in the name of reaching your goals. But you can still embrace a similar spirit.

Think of your career as a business. Your current employer is your primary customer. Your job, as the business owner, is to keep your customer happy so your business continues to grow and thrive. That's your responsibility and no one else's. How you do this is up to you, but it's not strictly what is listed on your job description. That's just the minimum expectation.

If you want to be a successful business owner, you need to think about why your customer hired you. How is *your* business supposed to help *their* business? What can you do to make sure you not only meet but exceed that goal? Most of the time, business owners don't have anyone telling them what to do—they have to get creative and figure it out. You can do the same thing. You don't need step-by-step instructions. If you know the result you want to achieve, always be on the lookout for new ways to make it happen.

At the same time, try to tap into your inner motivation for your business mission. It's not just about the job at hand; it's about fulfilling a greater purpose for your customer and for your career. Like any business owner, you're bound to encounter aspects of the work that are less than enjoyable. Don't lose sight of the big picture. The thing that separates the world's most successful entrepreneurs from the rest of the pack is their persistence. The more you dedicate to your business, the more you will get out of it.

Volunteer to Lead High-Profile Projects

For a lot of people, the idea of leading anything—be it a conga line at a friend's wedding or a major project at work—is daunting. As the leader, you have much greater visibility, both within the team and outside of it, which can be both risky and rewarding. As you've learned throughout this book, making yourself more visible is always a little uncomfortable, but I argue that the potential reward for leadership far outweighs the risk.

Most people avoid taking the lead on work projects, especially high-profile ones, for one simple reason: fear of failure. It's much safer to be a part of the team and let someone else take the lead. If things go awry, it's not your responsibility.

You can always throw your hands up and say, "Hey, I was just following the leader."

But that's a pretty cynical way to approach leadership, and this kind of attitude certainly won't make you anyone's favorite team member. After all, even if it's not technically your responsibility, you still want any project you're involved in to succeed, right? You're still going to work your tail off to make that happen, right?

Of course you are! So why hide in the shadows and let someone else take all the glory? Trust that you're a hard worker and a strong performer and, even if your leadership isn't perfect, you'll still give it the best you've got. Trust that people will see that and appreciate it.

When you volunteer to lead a project (meaning you're not "forced" to by virtue of your role), your visibility is automatically elevated. The fact that you're willing to accept the risk *voluntarily* shows that you're confident and you're also a team player. **Even if the project fails, these things remain true.**

It may be hard to believe, but being the leader of a failed project isn't necessarily a bad thing. People understand that some projects are ill-conceived and doomed no matter who the leader is. Even highly skilled leaders can't guarantee success 100% of the time; there are just too many variables, many of which are out of the leader's control.

What matters is that you're willing to toss your hat in the ring; you're willing to take responsibility for something bigger than yourself, even if that means possibly failing.

I want to help you manage your fear of failure, but I also recognize that failure is not the *desired* outcome. Obviously, when you take the lead on any project, high-profile or otherwise, you want to succeed. You want everyone on the team to do their part, and you want the project to achieve its stated objectives. You want to stay on budget and deliver on time.

Before you volunteer to take the lead on a project, make sure you're in the best possible position for success. Consider the project details and your proficiency in dealing with its various elements. As leader, you don't have to be an expert in all areas, but you should be able to offer meaningful contributions. Consider the people you will need to leverage and your established relationships. The more social capital you have with your team, the more effective your leadership is likely to be.

Be selective about the projects you volunteer to lead, but not so selective that you never make the leap. The more practice you get, the more you will continue to grow and refine your leadership skills.

Taking ownership of your work as described in this chapter not only elevates your visibility but also offers a wealth of other benefits. The more you are willing to think and act like an owner, the more you will be treated as an owner. This means more freedom and flexibility, more involvement and more influence.

When you combine these things, you'll be in an excellent position for advancement and other growth opportunities.

11

DEVELOP YOUR ONLINE PRESENCE

ny discussion of visibility would be incomplete without also examining the world's most powerful (and dangerous) tool for raising visibility: The Internet.

Today's technology can make you famous (or infamous) in a matter of minutes. With the help of your online presence, you can find a new job just as easily as you can lose your current one. You can establish credibility and demonstrate expertise just as quickly as you can become an embarrassing meme. Your judgment, for better or worse, is on full display when you post anything online—and you *will* be judged by others.

I have personally experienced the amazing power of the Internet in my own career. In 2006, while working as an executive assistant, I started a blog called "The Executive Assistant's Toolbox." I wanted to write about professional development, the many challenges of the EA role, and my experiences as I learned to navigate the business world as a young woman in my 20s.

I got the idea for the blog while climbing the StairMaster at the gym. A few hours later, I had published my first article on the topic of email etiquette. I went to sleep that night feeling excited about my new venture. When I woke up the next morning, my blog had more than 500 "subscribers." I was astonished. My boyfriend at the time assured me this was not normal. He had been writing a blog for years and had about 30 followers. Something had happened, but we didn't know what.

Later that day, after some investigating, we discovered that a popular blogger named Jay White (of DumbLittleMan.com) had, through a series of fortunate events, stumbled upon my article. After enjoying what he read and seeing that it was a brand-new blog, he had posted a message to his tens of thousands of subscribers asking them to go support a new, talented blogger. He had done this purely out of the kindness of his heart.

I sent him a gushing email of gratitude ... and to this day, I drop him a note about once a year to remind him of the incredible impact he had on my life.

You see, because of those 500-plus blog subscribers, I felt committed to continue. If I had struggled for years in obscurity, I might have gotten disenchanted with the whole thing. I might have given up. But instead, I kept writing and published a new article several times a week, and my subscriber number kept climbing.

I really didn't know why I was doing this. It was a lot of work, but I enjoyed it. I thought of it as a passion project— something that challenged me both intellectually and creatively. But I never had any idea that it would eventually alter my career path and change my life.

About a year and a half after I started the blog, I was approached by a startup out of Atlanta. The company was building a new online community for administrative professionals and wanted to talk to me about a possible partnership. About a month later, that company had purchased my blog—something I didn't even know you could do—and hired me to be the managing editor and community spokesperson for the new website.

Practically overnight, everything changed. I went from being an executive assistant with a passion project to being an "expert" in the administrative field. This phenomenon is known as "instant authority." When someone is positioned online as a leader in a community, the general public immediately grants them authority in that space. Because of this, I spent many years plagued by imposter syndrome. I never felt worthy of the credibility I had. People trusted me as a leader in the admin world, and I felt deeply unworthy of that trust.

What I eventually discovered was that my position in the community was built on relatability. People liked reading my articles because I wasn't afraid to share my insecurities, my challenges, and even my ignorance in certain areas. I also learned that my passion for personal and professional development helped motivate people to focus on their own growth. And I found that, because of my lifelong love of learning, I was a natural trainer and coach.

Over the years, I've obtained the education and experience I need to feel more comfortable with my position as a career expert. But make no mistake about it: My online presence did not always feel as authentic as it does today.

Unfortunately, the startup company in Atlanta did not succeed, but it gave me the platform to launch my new career and, in 2009, my new business and website, EatYourCareer.com. It's a funny name, I know. It's based on my belief that work can be an enriching and nourishing life experience. "Eat Your Career" is all about helping people achieve professional nourishment.

To this day, I have never paid for traditional advertising in my business. All the coaching and training work I do comes from people who follow my blog, or attend my free webinars, or have seen me present at various conferences. I am absolutely certain that, without the help of the Internet, I would not have this business and I might not have ever found my true career calling.

I share all of this to help you see that I really do understand the power of the online world. I believe a higher power of some sort guided me to this place. But I also believe that I have leveraged the heck out of the online tools at my disposal.

Everyone with an Internet connection has the ability to do the same thing. You can truly create the career you want for yourself. You can create opportunities you never knew possible. You can change your life.

It is beyond the scope of this book to discuss specific steps or recommendations for starting a blog or using any certain social media platform. Instead, this chapter will provide strategic guidance to help you create an online presence that enhances your professional visibility and supports your career goals.

Be Selective

The possibilities of the online world are countless and overwhelming. Every day, it seems, there's a new social media platform or website everyone is talking about, and it's just too much to keep up with. If you try to leverage them all, you'll inevitably do it poorly—as the saying goes, "Jack of all trades, master of none." Pick a handful to be a part of and don't even worry about the rest. At the time of this writing, LinkedIn is the only one I consider a must-have for professionals; everything else is optional.

Be Consistent

Whatever you choose to engage in, be sure to show a consistent brand across platforms. You don't want to confuse people by being a consummate professional on LinkedIn and then being a party animal over on Facebook. Chances are pretty good that people following you on one site will find you on others.

That's not to say you can't show more of your personal life on certain platforms. After all, they do serve different purposes. LinkedIn is a *professional* networking site and Facebook is a *social* networking site. Just make sure you're creating a cohesive —not conflicting—image of who you are and what you're all about.

Be Cautious

Building a strong online presence requires a hefty dose of good judgment.

We see examples nearly every day of people who fail to

understand the potentially life-altering consequences of posting inappropriate things for the world to see. If you post obscene, hateful things online—even in jest—or if you engage in any other disreputable behavior, you may have a very high price to pay for your poor judgement.

You have the freedom to post anything you'd like, but your employer also has the freedom to fire you for posting things that could reflect poorly on the company in the public eye. Don't fool yourself into thinking that privacy settings will protect you. Don't assume you can delete problematic posts without anyone being the wiser. If you put it online, expect that anyone and everyone can see it forever, including your current employer, prospective future employers, your grandmother, and your children.

If you're not proud of what you're putting out there, and you're not absolutely certain you can defend your choices, don't post it. If it's too late and it's already out there, delete it. People may still one day find it (because nothing is ever truly *gone*), but at least you'll make it more difficult.

You've heard this advice before; but it never fails to surprise me how many people don't heed these warnings. Please don't become a cautionary tale. Always, *always* think twice before posting anything.

Be Helpful

The Internet is all about connecting people and facilitating the free exchange of information. As an active participant in the online world, you have the ability to create a global network. You can learn from people all over the world, and they can learn from you.

As a general rule, I suggest that online tools are best used for deepening existing relationships and staying connected to real-life contacts, as opposed to forming *new* relationships. However, I know from personal experience that it is possible to create incredibly strong connections with people purely online —without ever meeting in "the real world." In fact, some of my best friends started out as online contacts, though we have met up in person many times since then.

The key with any online relationship (whether it exists solely in the virtual world or not) is to provide value through your interactions. We're all bombarded with information all day long; we don't want to add to the noise. Instead, we want to stand out as a helpful addition.

Whether your goal is to establish a new connection or simply stay top-of-mind with existing contacts, you want to be seen as a knowledgeable, useful person to know. To reiterate what you learned in Chapter 7 (Develop Meaningful Relationships), your strategy should always be to give first before requesting or expecting anything in return. In the online world, you can do this in a number of ways, including:

- **Post links to helpful articles, infographics, and other resources you find online:** Be sure to include your own analysis of the item or a few of the key highlights you found most interesting. That way, you're adding your own unique perspective, making the share even more valuable.
- **Pose a thoughtful question to inspire conversation with others:** Be sure to stay on top of the thread and respond back to people promptly. You don't want to come off as rude by making them feel ignored.

- **Write articles on topics relevant to your field, such as current trends, business events, and technological advances:** You can also share stories from your own personal experience, tips and tricks you've learned, and anything else that might prove useful to others. Writing is an effective way to establish yourself as a thought-leader for your field.
- **Join groups that align with your professional interests and become an active participant:** Contribute to the discussions by offering insight from your past work experience. Ask questions and provide answers of your own. The more frequently you engage in a meaningful way, the more people will begin to know, like, and trust you.

A compelling post can get shared, favorited, liked, or simply seen by a *lot* of people both inside and outside your immediate network. Some even take on a life of their own, becoming viral and generating thousands of views in a matter of hours. Don't count on that kind of response, but realize that it can happen.

The Internet enables a two-way conversation, so take advantage of it. *Interact* with people, don't just throw things at them. If you want to build a real relationship, online or otherwise, you have to engage in real, authentic dialogue. There's no reason that can't happen in the virtual world just as it does in the real one.

Be Persistent

It can take a while to get traction online. My story was a true anomaly. Most people spend years building up a following. But

I can assure you: Eventually, you will hit a tipping point at which things grow exponentially faster. Your job is to be persistent; don't give up when it feels like no one is listening. Just keep going.

Even a small online network can be valuable—sometimes, even *more* valuable than an extremely large one. Think quality over quantity.

Online Visibility for Job Search

Online visibility is especially important, and especially frustrating, when job searching. Online job applications have an average 4% response rate, which means that for every 100 submissions, you can expect about four interview invitations. With a well-crafted resume, you can increase that number a bit, but given the time required to complete an online application, that return hardly seems like a good investment.

That being said, I've certainly had some clients who found a job this way—and I have as well. But there are a lot of other online strategies you can leverage; take advantage of as many as possible. The more prevalent you are online, the easier it is for recruiters and hiring managers to find you.

Below, you'll find my top three suggestions to improve your online visibility specifically as it relates to job search:

1. Create a 100% complete LinkedIn profile

To experience all of the benefits of LinkedIn, you need an "All Star" profile, which means it's 100% complete. According to LinkedIn, users with the All Star status are 40 times more likely to receive opportunities through the platform. Approximately

94% of recruiters use LinkedIn to source and vet candidates, so this is crucial. When recruiters search to find prospective candidates that have specific qualifications, an All Star profile will appear at the top of their search results list. They are always more likely to reach out with opportunities to those who have active, robust profiles. The LinkedIn system will walk you through the steps required create a 100% complete profile.

Note: LinkedIn also offers a Premium account for job seekers that has a fee associated with it. It allows you to use special features and enjoy certain job search advantages. However, I do not recommend it for people who are not already fairly sophisticated LinkedIn users. In my experience, the free account is sufficient for most people.

2. Own your name domain

If it's not already taken, purchase your name domain immediately (for example, mine is ChrissyScivicque.com). It's a minimal investment—typically about $10—that pays off. If your name is already taken, add some words that help brand you and identify your profession or location (for example, JoeSmithWriter.com or JoeSmithDenver.com). Internet real estate is precious and it goes fast, so don't wait to do this.

More than 90% of employers screen prospective employees by searching online. When they enter your name into a search engine, you want *your* information and information within *your control* to land at the top of the results list. Obviously, this can be difficult if you have a very common name, but owning your name domain (or a version of it) will help ensure they can find you. Remember that sites like Facebook and LinkedIn also show up in search results, so once again, be sure everything you post is suitable for prospective employers to see.

Once you have the domain, you can use it to host any number of things that help build your credibility as a professional, such as:

- A blog that demonstrates your writing abilities and thought leadership
- A digital portfolio that displays samples of your work
- An online resume that provides deeper details of your work history and experience

3. Don't blast your network with generic requests

All too often, job seekers send out generic requests for help via mass email or social media post. For example, they say something like this: "Well, I'm back in the job market ... please let me know if you hear of anything!" This kind of thing is too vague to be meaningful, and it puts the onus on others to figure out what you want. Instead of blasting everyone at once with a less-than-useful message, connect with people directly and ask specifically for what you want—an introduction, a referral, etc. If you don't have a more specific request, at least let them know what kind of position you're seeking and what organizations you're targeting. Even if they can't provide direct assistance, they may know someone who can.

Just Get Started

The online world is here to stay, and in coming years, the role it plays in your career will only grow in importance.

Some people have difficulty accepting this fact. A former client of mine, Ella, had never created a social media account when we started working together. She was "philosophically" opposed to the idea, but as she entered her second year(!) of job searching, she also understood that her belief system wasn't doing her any favors.

I spent several months convincing Ella that she needed to take small but crucial steps to create an online presence; without it, she simply couldn't compete in today's market. I had to explain that, when recruiters and hiring managers can't find any trace of you online, they get suspicious. When a so-called "professional" doesn't have a LinkedIn profile, they assume there's a reason—you're probably hiding something.

Ella wasn't shying away from the online world for any nefarious reason. She simply didn't want to participate. It required learning new technology, and that was always a pain. But it also felt invasive. She didn't want to share all her intimate details with strangers. Plus, she was already so busy! All of these online platforms seemed to be built for wasting time.

Ella had a lot of valid reasons for her absence online, and perhaps you relate. But let me tell you what I told her: You can do it in the way that feels right for *you*. You don't have to share intimate details if you don't want to, and you don't have to let it consume hours of your life. You can figure out the technology, I promise. Even just doing the bare minimum is better than nothing at all.

The longer you wait to get involved, the more difficult it will become. You'll build it up in your head to be this big, overwhelming beast. Just get started and be intentional about how you approach it. Take it one step at a time and don't worry about what everyone else is doing. Find a way that feels good *for you*.

12

EXHIBIT IMPECCABLE INTEGRITY

M any years ago, in my early 20s, I worked at a bank. One day, a co-worker arrived at the office and asked if I had heard what happened at the branch right down the road from us. As she described it, the entire staff had been fired that morning for alleged theft and fraud. Apparently, investigators had been reviewing security footage for weeks and found clear and repeated violations of bank policy ... and much worse.

I remember this day vividly because, in a single breath, everything I thought about the staff at that branch changed. I had known these people for several years. I had respected them. Suddenly, they were strangers. It was a perfect example of the famous Warren Buffett quote: "It takes 20 years to build a reputation and five minutes to ruin it."

This event sparked a pretty significant point in my own life. When this happened, I found myself engaging in some rather uncomfortable self-evaluation. If people were watching me on security camera footage, what would they see? I wasn't just thinking about clear black-and-white matters of policy and law. I thought about my interactions with colleagues and clients, my day-to-day choices. Was I truly handling confidential information appropriately? Was I respecting the detailed nature of my job? Or was I skimping on little things because I thought no one would notice?

I had to take a good, hard look at my actions and ask myself, "Am I proud?"

It turns out, I wasn't particularly proud, and that's how I knew I had a problem.

I believe everyone has a conscience—that little voice that tells you when something is right or wrong. But too many times, we suppress what we hear. We do this for all kinds of reasons. Maybe we think, in the moment, it makes life easier. Maybe we think it's no big deal. Maybe we think no one will ever know.

But here's my experience: I can't escape myself. Even if I'm the only one who knows, I can't live with the guilt and self-disappointment of integrity issues. At the end of the day, I want to be able to look at myself in the mirror and feel good about my actions. That's the only way I can sleep well at night.

I used to think about this a lot when I would walk my dog. She would inevitably do her business in a neighbor's yard. If it was cold out or if I was tired, I would find myself immediately looking around to see whether anyone was watching. It was like a little devil on my shoulder was saying, "You don't have to pick that up! No one is around! Why take your gloves off? Why bother bending over and then finding a trash can? You can totally get away with leaving it right there!"

Then, my better angels would remind me: Integrity is about

doing the right thing even when no one is watching. Sure, it's a small indiscretion to leave my dog's business in someone else's yard. But that's not the point. I wouldn't want someone leaving their dog's business in my yard. I want to be a good neighbor. I want to live in a respectful community where we all take care of each other's property. Why would I sacrifice that for a minute of laziness?

It doesn't matter if it's a perceived "small" lapse of integrity. To me, it all adds up. A few small lapses throughout the day, and suddenly, I'm not happy with who I am as a person. And when that happens, I'm more likely to continue making bad decisions and less likely to bring my best to the world.

In the workplace, integrity should be considered your most precious asset; it's more important than your strong reputation, your powerful relationships, or the results you achieve. Without it, these things aren't even possible. Once it's lost, it can be nearly impossible to regain. Just as the staff members of that bank branch can attest, it can cost you your job ... and so much more. Lack of integrity can put you in the world's most powerful spotlight. It's the kind of visibility no one wants.

Defining Ethics

The law is black and white: We have a specific set of rules that we agree as a society to abide by. When one of these rules is broken, there can be legal ramifications. Bernie Madoff, for example, was an investor who famously ran a "Ponzi scheme," and ultimately defrauded thousands of clients out of billions of dollars. He broke the law, and because he did, he is now serving prison time.

Ethics, like the law, is an *external* system of rules and

procedures. Usually there are rewards when we follow the rules and punishments when we break them.

Ethics overlaps with the law but also presents a whole additional territory that's harder to define. Acting ethically is not *only* about acting within the law. It's also about acting within the "spirit" of the law, and abiding by the established principles within yourself and your organization, which may not be specifically spelled out within the law.

Your personal ethics in the workplace are influenced by your personal values as well as the organization's values. When we choose to work for an organization, we are agreeing to adopt their code of conduct. The organization's values become a part of the fabric of our own ethics.

Your integrity (or lack thereof) inspires you to act ethically or not. Integrity is an *internal* system of principles that guides our behavior. The rewards are intrinsic—a feeling of strength and wholeness. Integrity is a choice rather than an obligation. When we act with integrity, we do what is right, even when no one is watching, because it is rewarding in and of itself.

The Impact of Ethical Lapses

Ethical lapses can have far-reaching effects, as illustrated in the following graphic.

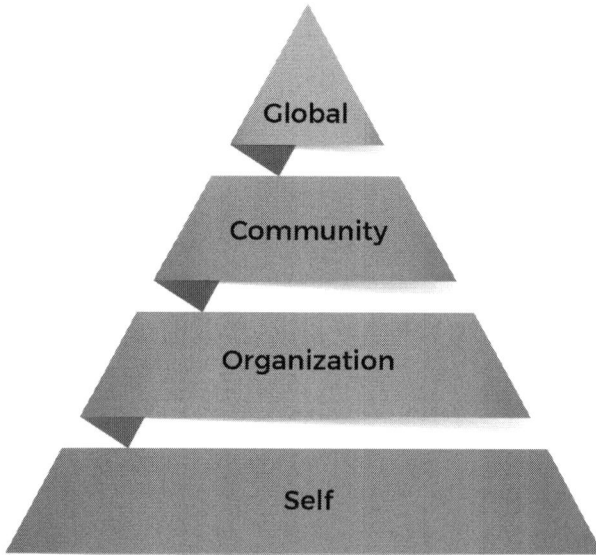

The impact to **self** can be dramatic, including personal stress and anxiety. This is caused by what's known as "cognitive dissonance," which happens when actions are not aligned with beliefs. Most people acting unethically are aware of this conflict, if not consciously then subconsciously, and thus cognitive dissonance is sparked. We know better, and yet we still act in a way that conflicts with our knowledge.

The impact to the **organization** can also be dramatic. An organization relies on its people to uphold certain standards of behavior. When we join the team, we are implicitly (and sometimes explicitly) agreeing to these standards. When we fail to live up to them, the organization can suffer in a variety of ways—reputations can be destroyed, profitability can be harmed, the people within the organization can suffer, and so on. Ultimately, ethical lapses have even been the complete downfall of entire organizations, causing them to crumble under their weight.

Enron is a powerful example of this. Widely considered one of the most innovative and successful companies of the 1990s, Enron came crashing down when it was discovered that the employees had engaged in a wide array of fraudulent accounting activities to hide the company's dire financial reality. The tactics were described as deceptive, bewildering, creative, systematic and institutionalized—meaning, these activities were essentially a part of the company's normal business operations. As all of this was discovered, Enron's stock plummeted, costing investors billions of dollars. When the firm declared bankruptcy in 2001, thousands of people lost their jobs.

Ethical lapses can impact the entire **community** and can have **global** ramifications. In the 2007-08 financial crisis, our entire economy was brought to its knees because of the unethical behavior of people in the banking, investment, and mortgage industries. Ethical lapses created an atmosphere of "anything goes." Many unsuspecting homeowners became overleveraged because of what's now known as "predatory lending." Mortgage professionals took advantage of their clients' ignorance to give them loans they likely couldn't handle. This was a major contributing factor in the housing bubble that later burst and resulted in millions of foreclosures and upside-down mortgages. The ramifications of that unethical behavior impacted our entire global economy, local communities, business organizations, and millions of individual lives.

Ethics and Integrity in the Workplace

Ethics and integrity touch every aspect of our personal and professional lives. We make choices every day regarding our interactions with these things—we either act in a way that aligns with our ethical principles or which conflicts with them.

- **With our colleagues:** We hear things, we see things, we speak to people, we engage with them. Our behavior can either uphold our own values and the organization's, or it can detract from them.
- **Finances:** You probably touch a variety of things that impact the financial security of your company every day. Perhaps you have a company credit card. Maybe you are responsible for purchasing or you have the authority to get reimbursed for certain business-related expenses. The wrong decisions could have a direct impact on the financial health of your organization.
- **Property:** We all have company property within our possession onsite and perhaps off. Computers, information, supplies, and equipment whose purpose is to help us do the work. Taking that property and using it for other purposes is a common lapse of ethical judgment.
- **Clients:** As an employee, you are a representative of your organization. Your interactions with clients are a reflection of your own values and the organization's. If you lie to clients or engage with them in an unethical way, the organization suffers; it gets a bad reputation or the client leaves.

- **Time:** We are all on company time when we're
  working. We're entrusted to use that time wisely.
  Leaving early and getting paid for that time, for
  example, represents an ethical lapse. Being "on the
  clock" but not actually working is known as time
  theft. According to the American Payroll
  Association, the average employee steals four hours
  and five minutes every week, which is staggering.
  This costs U.S. employers $20 billion to $40 billion
  in lost productivity each year.

Note: I tend to believe that time theft estimates are exaggerated. After all, an employee who is on the clock and chatting with co-workers in the breakroom is not necessarily stealing time. He or she may be engaging in valuable team building. An employee who quickly checks his or her cell phone for a text from their kid isn't necessarily stealing time; they're being human. These kinds of activities are absolutely acceptable within reason. I think they only become problematic with too much frequency, which is a judgment call based on organizational culture.

- **Confidentiality:** Within our organizations, we all are
  privy to certain information that isn't made public.
  Sharing these things inappropriately can have
  serious impact on competition and even on the
  value of the company.
- **Quality of Work:** We are all being paid to perform a
  job. When the quality of that job isn't up to standard,
  we're not upholding our end of the agreement we
  made with our employer.

Navigating Ethical Dilemmas

A former coaching client of mine, Joe, was a project manager at a software development company. Joe was working on a project with a small team to develop a specific piece of software for their client. The project was complicated and intense and had a tight deadline and budget.

Joe discovered along the way that corners were being cut to meet those tight parameters. It became clear to him that the intention of the team was to provide a subpar product to the client. Joe knew the product would not meet their client's expectations; they had promised something different than what they were going to deliver.

Joe was conflicted because he knew that, in order to deliver the product they had promised, it couldn't be done within the budget and timeline the organization had agreed to. So, he was pulled in two different directions: The organization's value for delivering within the client's time and budget parameters, and his own value for providing a high-quality product, were in conflict. The rest of the team wanted to honor one side of the equation at the cost of the other. This represented a classic ethical dilemma for Joe.

In the short-term, if they met the deadline and budget parameters, they would fulfill their obligation, but in the long-term the client wouldn't be happy with the product. They would figure out what had happened and likely wouldn't use Joe's company again.

Ethical dilemmas often arise from short-term thinking and conflicts in priorities. Our job is to measure the value of each against the long-term landscape to determine the appropriate course of action.

After repeatedly voicing his concerns to the team and not getting anywhere, Joe finally took his concerns to the client. He explained where things stood and what would truly be needed to get the job done right. He gave the client two options: We can keep the deadline and budget as they are, and this is what we can deliver; or we can change the deadline and budget, and deliver what you really want.

The client was frustrated, of course, but understood the situation. The client heard what Joe was saying and agreed to the new specifications. In the end, the client was satisfied with the work, and the experience with the organization was far better than the alternative.

Is this the right approach for everyone? Maybe not. But for Joe, speaking to the client directly was the right decision, and it paid off. He felt he was able to act with integrity, and ultimately, both he and the organization were better off for it.

This is an example of the two sides of integrity: It entails managing your own behavior to ensure you're acting in accordance with your own ethical principles, as well as addressing the behavior of others when they are engaging in potentially dangerous lapses of judgment. You don't have to be some kind of ethics watchdog, but you do have an obligation to uphold the standards set forth by your company. When you see something that poses a potentially imminent and substantive threat to the organization or team, you should act.

What constitutes a "substantive" threat is subjective.

If you see someone pocket a pack of Post-it Notes, you might not automatically see that as an imminent and substantive threat. A pack of Post-its isn't going to bring down your company. It could be an oversight—a thoughtless action that doesn't really represent a threat. You have no idea if this person has some professional business to take care of at home that requires a pack of Post-its.

Or it could be a pattern of behavior. A pack of Post-its one day, a piece of computer equipment the next. That might be a different story. That represents a potentially imminent and substantive threat. Not only is the value much more significant, but it also could contain confidential information. It could be a major breach of security. That would likely be something to get involved with. You still don't know if there's legitimate business for it, but you may need to inquire at this point because of the significant *potential* level of the threat.

It's always a judgment call. Inquiring is always okay. You likely don't have all the facts in any situation you observe from the outside. But if something sparks concern, you have the right to ask about it. Does this at times create uncomfortable questions for others to answer? Yes. But if nothing wrong is happening, the questions are no big deal. It's only when something is being hidden that it's seen as disruptive.

A good friend, Mark, once told me about an ethical dilemma he faced a few years back: At a new company, some colleagues gave Mark some "tips" for essentially padding his expense reports to get money reimbursed that he wasn't entitled to. Mark was tempted; it seemed like everyone was doing it. This was an unspoken "acceptable" thing to do—get creative and you can make a little extra bonus cash here and there.

But Mark didn't give in to that temptation. He honored his own values and the values of the organization, and he reported only the legitimate expenses. Still, he knew others were continuing to do this. He heard about it. He witnessed it. It was spoken about freely. He ignored it for a long time, and it ate at him. Mark started looking at his colleagues as thieves. He started thinking about the bigger impact of their actions—how that money they were stealing was money that could have gone toward a rightly deserved bonus.

Mark slowly began to see what he originally considered as an ethical lapse as a legal breach, and he finally reported it to his HR department. The company began to enforce much stricter policies and an investigation was pursued. Mark was kept out of it, but of course, several people suspected he started the commotion. That didn't bother him, though. His trust for these people was already destroyed, and his trust in the organization was slowly being rebuilt as he saw the company do the right thing.

Some ethical matters are black and white; others have many shades of gray. A variety of things might happen in the workplace that you don't like. You might find certain behavior highly unsavory. It might violate your personal values, but it might not be something that puts the organization or the team in imminent and substantive danger. Whether you address such things will always be a judgment call.

Addressing Ethical Lapses

If and when you witness an ethical issue and determine it's necessary to get involved, be careful in choosing to whom you address your concerns. Generally, the more people you involve, the more difficult the situation becomes.

Human resources is generally the guardian for these kinds of concerns, but many people distrust HR. Here's what you need to realize: HR professionals are specifically trained to handle these kinds of concerns. It's a primary function of their role. They are looking at it from the point of view of protecting the organization and staying on the right side of the law.

They are, however, bound to certain requirements. They can't, for example, always keep your disclosure of concerns confidential. They won't typically just take note of what you tell them without doing their due diligence to look into the situation. You may be required to participate in investigations down the road, whether you want to or not.

Once you take a concern to HR, it is out of your hands.

In my earlier story, Joe chose to take his concerns directly to his client. He tried going to his teammates, but ultimately, he was a project manager, so it was his responsibility. He had an obligation to the client and to the organization, and he made a choice based on his circumstance. Figuring out who to talk to and how to approach it is rarely an easy, clear-cut decision.

However, don't sit on information for too long. Once you know that something unethical is happening, you're involved. Get it off your plate by voicing your concerns. And remember, you don't need *all* the facts. You are not an investigator. You are not the jury or the judge. You are simply a witness acknowledging what you *do* know, or acknowledging questions or concerns. This is absolutely your right and responsibility.

I'll offer one additional suggestion: Keep written documentation of what happened, who you spoke to, and when you spoke. Some ethical situations can get really ugly. You need to protect yourself.

Embracing Personal Integrity

In my experience, most people *want* to have integrity. They try not to lie or steal or cheat. But these things *do* happen in the workplace all the time. Usually, it starts much smaller and grows bigger over time. That's why you have to be vigilant with your behaviors. The more you allow "small" misdeeds, the less they will bother you. Over time, it will become easier and easier to silence that inner voice telling you your actions are wrong. It's a slippery slope.

An executive mentor of mine once told me that his boss, in the early part of his career, asked him to lie on his behalf. My mentor told him, "If I can lie *for* you, I can lie *to* you. And I don't want to be that person."

To me, that's a strong statement. We can't be unethical on some things, in some situations, for some people, and expect that it won't cause damage. It will, whether we know it in the moment or not.

People are *always* watching and listening. Everything you do (or don't do) contributes to the perceptions they have about your character. This is one reason I encourage everyone to engage in careful conversations in the workplace. Realize that things can be misinterpreted.

Too many people think they can get away with certain ethical lapses in the workplace. They gossip about others, take credit for work that's not theirs, fail to follow through on promises, and so on. They fool themselves into believing these are not true questions of integrity—but of course, they are. They wrongly believe such behavior goes unnoticed or is tacitly accepted. Then, they wonder why their career has stalled out, why they can't get a promotion, why they aren't recognized or rewarded in the way they believe is deserved.

There's not always an *immediate* consequence, but a lack of integrity will inevitably catch up with you. Some call it "karma," but I don't think there's anything mystical about it. What you put out into the world is always reflected back.

So, how do you manage your own behavior to ensure you're embracing personal integrity? Here are some questions to consider:

- **"Are my actions aligned with my values and the values of the organization?"** What do your behaviors demonstrate about you and your company? Are you actually living in a way that honors what you say you believe? Are you working in a way that honors what your organization aspires to be?
- **"What are my motives?"** What is driving your decisions? Are you propelled by self-interest and greed? Are you focused solely on fulfilling your needs without regard for the impact it may have on others? Or are you motivated by something bigger than yourself?
- **"If others knew of my behaviors, what would they think?"** True integrity is doing the right thing even when others aren't looking. But this is still a good gauge to measure by. What if they *were* looking? Would you act differently?
- **"Am I contributing to the long-term health of the team and organization, or am I detracting from it?"** Ethical decisions—even hard ones that seem to go against the consensus—will ultimately contribute more to the company and to your team than unethical ones. Integrity builds a sustainable future; don't be shortsighted in your choices.

- **"Am I proud of my behavior?"** Can you sleep
  soundly at night knowing your behaviors? Can you
  stand behind your choices? Can you look yourself in
  the eye and say, "I let my better angels guide me
  today"?

INTEGRITY IS easy to discount when you've never experienced the other side. If you've only been surrounded by people who have it, you may not understand just how glaring it is when it's missing. If you've never been challenged by situations that put your own integrity at risk, you may not know just how quickly it can be impaired or lost altogether.

However, most people know these things all too well.

I encourage you to protect your integrity with everything you have. Examine yourself critically and continuously. Hold yourself to the highest standards. Others already hold you to those same standards, even if they don't necessarily say as much. Don't disappoint them ... or yourself.

13

CONCLUSION

A t the end of 2011, when my business was just 2 years old, I moved from Atlanta, GA to Denver, CO. A cross-country move is hard enough, but hauling a baby business to another state is exponentially more stressful. I knew I had to hit the ground running to make sure I stayed afloat.

Just a few months after I arrived, a contact of mine (fellow career coach and corporate trainer, Bud Bilanich) introduced me to Nancy, the producer of our local morning show, *Good Day Colorado*. Nancy was looking for someone to appear on the show the next week to discuss common issues facing job seekers in the Denver metro area. She asked if I'd be interested.

I would have been a fool to pass up the opportunity for free television advertising in my new city! But, when I got the offer, the first thing that came to mind was, "I need to lose 20 pounds first."

Thankfully, I didn't say that. I simply said "yes" and vowed to find a flattering top that would hide the extra weight I was carrying at the time.

Let me just say this: I am not a natural on TV. I feel very stiff and uncomfortable, and anyone who knows me in real life could see that. The segment was only about three minutes long, but I've never felt more nervous in my life. I spent the entire week prior practicing what I wanted to say and how I would say it.

When it was finally over, Nancy walked me out of the studio, and I just remember feeling a massive, overwhelming sense of relief. Then, she asked me to do it again the next week. I could hardly believe my own ears when I heard myself say "yes."

To make a long story short, I was a featured career expert on *Good Day Colorado* for nearly two years. It never really got easier or more comfortable. I can't even say I particularly enjoyed the work. But I am incredibly grateful for it nonetheless.

I think this experience illustrates much of what has been discussed in this book. This opportunity only came about because of my relationship with Bud and the fact that he trusted me enough to make the introduction to Nancy. It was only meant to be a small, one-time thing, but I took it seriously. And because I really gave it my best, I was invited to do more.

Visibility-raising opportunities don't always take the form we desire, and they don't necessarily appear exactly when we want them. They also don't appear out of nowhere. We aren't just handed opportunities for no reason. They are the result of all the little things we've done up to that point.

In the future, you may find yourself granted an opportunity to do something far outside your comfort zone—to work on an exciting high-profile project, for example, or to take on a major promotion. You may feel undeserving and ill-prepared. You may fear the visibility that will inevitably come with taking this next big step in your career. It is my hope that you will do it anyway.

It is quite likely that, if you follow the advice in this book, you will face these kinds of situations repeatedly in your career. The more you do to raise your visibility, the more opportunities you will receive to raise it even more. I assure you: Whatever comes your way is *deserved*. The reputation you've built, the results you've achieved, and the relationships you've developed make these opportunities possible.

There's always another level of success beyond your current one, even if you can't begin to imagine what that could look like. I always tell people, "If I had mapped out what might be possible in my career back in my 20s, I would have sold myself massively short."

I had no idea I could ever run a business, write a book, speak on live television, or present my own original training material to thousands of people around the world. The opportunities found me because I put myself in the right position to be found.

This point was really driven home for me in 2018. I was asked to speak at the International Association for Administrative Professionals (IAAP) Summit, one of the largest conferences for admins in the world. I joined the attendees one morning to watch a keynote speaker named Dr. Veronica Cochran. At the time, she had just been named the new CEO of the association.

During her presentation, Dr. Cochran shared a powerful analogy. The following transcript is shared with her permission.

If I had an incredible Picasso painting and I put the painting in the basement and I said to you, "Come over to my house!" and I gave you a tour of all of my home, and I took you in the basement, and then I brought you back upstairs to the kitchen and sat you down and I said to you, "Did you see my Picasso?" You would probably say, "Where?"

Because it wasn't positioned in the right light.

*Your job is to position yourself in the right light—to showcase your talent, your strength, your expertise. Nobody has to ask you for that. You **showcase** that.*

To me, this perfectly sums up everything we're talking about here. You are a masterpiece. It's your responsibility to help people see that. Positioned in the right light, people and opportunities will be drawn to you. Hidden away in the dark, you're bound to stay that way.

With this book, it is my goal to help you become The Obvious Choice. When opportunities arise—whether for promotions, exciting projects, or anything else—I want you to be the top contender. When raises need to be allocated, I want your name to spring to mind as the most deserving employee. When people are searching for professionals with your skills, I want them to find you.

I want you to never again feel the isolation, inferiority, and injustice of being invisible at work. You have all the tools you need to position the masterpiece that is you in the right light. What you do from here will determine how your career unfolds. If you do the work, I honestly believe you will create something beyond your wildest dreams.

It happened for me. It will happen for you.

ABOUT THE AUTHOR

Chrissy Scivicque (pronounced "Civic") is a certified coach, trainer and consultant specializing in professional development and career advancement. She provides education and support for individuals and teams to help elevate workplace performance and increase career satisfaction.

Chrissy is a certified Professional Career Manager (PCM) and has completed over 100 hours of CTI core curriculum for life coaches. She holds a Bachelor's Degree in Marketing from Sonoma State University in California and has obtained

Training and Instructional Design certification from the Association for Talent Development.

Chrissy has developed and delivered training for some of the world's most recognized companies including Accenture, Capital One, Northrop Grumman, Microsoft, W.W. Grainger, TIAA-CREF, Georgia Power, GoDaddy, Turner Broadcasting, Eastman Chemical, and more. Working in coordination with stakeholders in the organization, Chrissy helps define desired business outcomes and creates measurable, positive results with her work.

A former career expert for U.S. News & World Report, Chrissy's work is regularly featured in a variety of print and online publications. She has published over 500 articles on career-related topics and is the author of the book, "The Proactive Professional."

Chrissy lives in Denver, CO where she served as the featured career expert on *Good Day Colorado* for 2 years.

Learn more about Chrissy by visiting EatYourCareer.com.

ALSO BY CHRISSY SCIVICQUE

The Proactive Professional

Build Your Professional Development Plan Workbook

Digital Products and Programs available exclusively on EatYourCareer.com

Personal Branding for Professional Success

Resume & Cover Letter Toolkit

Rock Your Interview

Build Your Professional Portfolio

Networking Naturally

Guide to Goal Setting & Goal Getting

Modern Business Etiquette

F.I.N.D. Your Nourishing Career

G.R.O.W. Your Nourishing Career

Job Seeker Jump Start

Onsite Coaching & Training Programs

ELEVATE Admins

Next Wave Leaders

Custom programs available

THE CAREER SUCCESS LIBRARY

LEARN | ACHIEVE | TRANSFORM

Made in the USA
Middletown, DE
26 September 2021